zodiac

enhance your life through astrology

nicholas
campion

DEDICATION

To my parents, Ruth and Desmond, who started me on this journey.

Editorial Director: Jane O'Shea

Creative Director: Mary Evans

Art Director: Françoise Dietrich

Project Editor: Hilary Mandleberg

Art Editor: Rachel Gibson

Production: Julie Hadingham

Picture Research: Nadine Bazar

Picture Assistant: Sarah Airey

First published in 2000 by Quadrille Publishing Limited

Alhambra House

27–31 Charing Cross Road

London WC2H 0LS

British Library Cataloguing-in-Publication Data

A catalogue record for this book is available from the British Library.

ISBN 1 902757 43 2

Printed and bound by Star Standard Industries (Pte) Ltd

zodiac

contents

introduction

THERE ARE FEW SIGHTS AS MARVELLOUS AS A DARK SKY LIBERALLY SPRINKLED WITH GLISTENING STARS AND WITH THE THICK WHITE STREAM OF THE MILKY WAY STRETCHING FROM ONE HORIZON TO THE OTHER. EVER SINCE HUMAN BEINGS FIRST GAZED AT THEM, THE HEAVENS HAVE INSPIRED THE DREAMS OF POETS, ARTISTS, SCIENTISTS AND MYSTICS. FROM THE WONDERS OF THE NIGHT SKY TO THE RISING SUN OR THE APPEARANCE OF THE CRESCENT MOON IN EARLY EVENING, THE CELESTIAL BODIES HAVE SERVED AS SOURCES OF SCIENTIFIC WISDOM, METAPHORS FOR LOVE AND SYMBOLS OF THE SPLENDOUR OF GOD'S CREATION.

NATURE'S RHYTHMS CREATE ENDLESS AWE AND WONDER. NIGHT FOLLOWS DAY AND THE SEASONS FLOW WITH AN UNSHAKEABLE INEVITABILITY THAT IS ESSENTIAL TO LIFE ON EARTH. THE SUN IS THE SOURCE OF OUR HEAT AND LIGHT; EVERY ATOM IN OUR BODIES WAS CREATED IN ITS WHITE-HOT CORE. TRULY, WE ARE CHILDREN OF THE COSMOS.

Astrology raises many questions about our relationship with the universe. Astrologers tend to think of the cosmos as one integrated whole in which consciousness and matter are interdependent and all parts of the universe are linked, no matter how far apart they are. As it happens, this is a point of view entirely in tune with modern views of the environment, which have come full circle, back to the primitive belief that all natural systems are interrelated. It is an idea that was summed up by Islamic mystics in the phrase, 'As above, so below and as below, so above' and also stands at the heart of the philosopher Leibnitz's argument that God is the universe and the universe is God.

But every student of astrology has to learn the distinction between, on the one hand, natural astrology – the study of real celestial influences and causes and the ancestor of modern astrophysics – and, on the other, judicial astrology. In judicial astrology the astrologer, as the term implies, has to reach a judgement. Judicial astrology is, overwhelmingly, the astrology we encounter nowadays in magazine horoscopes or in the astrologer's consulting room. It is an interpretative art, not an exact science, concerned not with measurement but with meaning.

Judicial astrology deals less with notions of cause and effect than with human values, and the sensitive astrologer will listen to an individual's concerns rather than mapping out a future set in stone. In fact, most professional astrologers nowadays pay far less attention to predicting the future than they do to encouraging their clients to understand themselves. If, the theory runs, we work out why we do the things we do, then we can improve our behaviour and take control of our future, thus making the giving of predictions redundant. The question to ask an astrologer is not 'What am I like?' but 'What can I do?', for every sign of the zodiac contains an element of liberation, each has a character which it can transcend and everyone is born into circumstances which he or she can change. Thus the emphasis is on enhancing free will rather than succumbing to fate. We can learn to recognise the way we are but not necessarily accept it. If you are looking for a modern astrological motto, you could do no better than the words, 'Know thyself'.

Astrology and relationships

What frequently lies behind someone's first visit to an astrologer is a desire for change. Often a client's relationships are in the firing line: he or she may be finding these inhibiting and may think that they are preventing their own personal growth. Astrology is well suited to providing valuable insights. The characteristics of the zodiac signs in our chart can be seen as representing different facets of our personality – perhaps even sub-personalities. During a chart consultation, the astrologer will look at these and will discuss their function in different parts of our lives and at different moments. One facet might be dominant at work, another at home, and so on.

Insights like these are especially helpful when it comes to trying to understand our relationships, especially those in which it seems as if we have no control over our emotions. Such relationships may feel as if they were made in heaven or we may feel that we cannot stand the sight of the other person. Astrology will help us find out why we were attracted or repelled in the first place, and once we can observe ourselves in this more objective manner, we can truly start making our own decisions about our relationships with others. This is the first step towards stopping blaming other people, in any walk of life, for our problems. It does not mean that we are responsible for everything that happens to us, only that we can control our responses.

Astrologers and psychologists go further still. They suggest that people come into our lives at particular moments to fulfil special functions. Sometimes it even feels as if we conjure up certain individuals when we need them. Thus some relationships seem to be destined or doomed by fate, as was the case with Romeo and Juliet, Shakespeare's 'star-crossed lovers'.

Any unexpected love affair or dramatic dispute can be seen as part of our own inner journey, the process we go through in order to learn about ourselves and discover what we are capable of. Our relationships therefore often entail a voyage of discovery. As long as we remember that we may need other people to fulfil a purpose of which we are not yet aware, and that we may not feel the same tomorrow as we do today, we will begin to understand ourselves – and our partners.

Drawing up a birth chart

So what happens if you go to see an astrologer? The astrologer's first step, before a consultation can take place, is to take the client's time, date and place of birth. With this information, a birth chart – or horoscope – is drawn up that maps, in relation to the twelve signs of the zodiac, the positions of the Sun, Moon and planets as they were seen from Earth at that time and place. The birth sign – or Sun sign – is the sign of the zodiac in which the Sun is found at birth. However, the calculation of our calendar is complicated by many considerations, including the fact that the Earth spins on its axis once a day and orbits around the Sun once a year. In addition, there are various minor wobbles to take into account. As a result, the Sun does not enter each sign of the zodiac on the same day every year, so astrologers usually give an average date for the beginning and end of each Sun sign. That is why, if you were born at the very end of one sign or the start of the next, you may find discrepancies in the horoscopes you read.

Then, no matter where the Sun is at the time of birth, the planets (the Moon, Mercury, Venus, Mars, Jupiter, Saturn, Uranus, Neptune and Pluto) – each of which has a range of meanings – will be spread out through all the other signs, so it is quite possible to be born with five or six planets in a sign other than the birth sign. So, when astrologers talk about people being Arien or Taurean, they can mean that they have other planets in those signs, not necessarily the Sun.

While the birth, or Sun, sign is the one that popular horoscopes go by, the sign containing the Moon at the moment of your birth is at least as significant, for while the Sun is said to reflect your inner self and the deeper aspects of your identity, the Moon may reveal your emotional reactions to circumstances. So it follows that if you read about your Moon sign as well as your Sun sign (see pages 16–19), you will get a more rounded picture of your character and personality.

Finally, the astrologer inserts in the birth chart twelve divisions – called 'houses' – based on the horizon. These twelve houses rule specific areas of life, such as work or relationships. According to the 'house' in which each planet falls, that planet's meaning is then applied to that area of life.

And so it is that every stage along the twelve-fold journey through the zodiac is relevant to each of us. Ancient prints show models of human beings with the zodiac signs imprinted on their bodies, indicating that we all, metaphorically, contain all twelve signs. In other words, the zodiac is a complete picture of human experience.

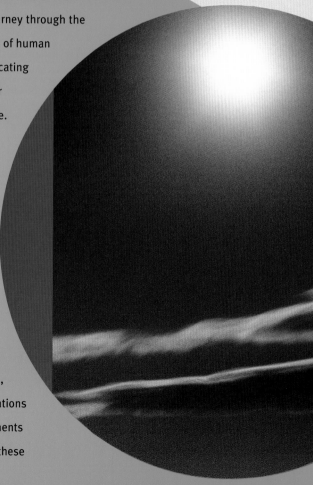

Finding the real you

It is clear then, that astrologers add layer after layer of complexity to each horoscope. In addition, the birth chart is far from static. The patterns it contains begin to change within minutes of birth and the precise condition of any horoscope at any time of day is assessed using factors that can alter from every fifteen minutes to every hundred years. We no longer end up being grouped under twelve types. Instead we emerge as unique individuals.

When it comes to understanding these myriad factors, each has a standard interpretation that describes ideal situations or textbook cases. Many of these contain contradictory elements or overlap with elements in other people's horoscopes. But these interpretations are not intended as accounts of what we are like. They are there to encourage us to weigh up our strengths and weaknesses, to see ways to take responsibility for our own decisions, to gain a clearer understanding of our actions, to better our lives and to improve our relationships. They help us to look not just at who we are, but at who we could be.

Astrology is therefore dynamic. It assumes that we are all in a continual state of flux. No day is the same as any other, no two individuals are exactly alike, and we all experience constantly fluctuating emotions and circumstances. We are travellers through space and time.

Interpreting the zodiac

Zodiac is a Greek word meaning 'pertaining to animals' or, sometimes, 'circle of animals'. It shares the same root as the word 'zoo'. The zodiac used by Western astrologers was developed over a period of several thousand years, mainly by the Babylonians – and perhaps by even earlier people – but has had some additions made by the Egyptians and Greeks. There are different zodiacs, but the best known are the tropical zodiac and the sidereal zodiac.

The tropical zodiac is the one used by Western astrologers. It consists of the twelve zodiac signs and is based on the seasons and equinoxes and on a sky divided into twelve segments of equal size. The Sun always enters Aries, the first sign of the zodiac, on 21 March. In the northern hemisphere, this is the spring equinox; in the southern, it is the autumn equinox.

The sidereal zodiac – from the Latin *sidus*, meaning 'star' – is based on the stars. There are two main types of sidereal zodiac – the one used by astronomers and the one used by Indian astrologers. That used by astronomers is based entirely on the stars and consists of constellations of different sizes. It is not used for astrology, only for describing the positions of the planets.

The sidereal zodiac used by Indian astrologers is split into twelve divisions of equal size. As the stars have gradually shifted their positions in relation to the seasons, so the Indian and Western zodiacs have diverged, and a horoscope cast in India will provide different information to one cast in the West.

The Qualities

The Western zodiac signs are divided into three Qualities – Cardinal, Fixed and Mutable – which influence the character of each sign. Signs of the same Quality share the same characteristics. Thus the Cardinal signs – Aries, Cancer, Libra and Capricorn – are all assertive and like to control their environment; the Fixed signs – Taurus, Leo, Scorpio and Aquarius – all resist change; the Mutable signs – Gemini, Virgo, Sagittarius and Pisces – are all flexible.

The Elements

Similarly, the signs are divided into four Elements – Fire, Earth, Air and Water – which, like the Qualities, influence the character of each sign. Again, signs of the same Element share the same characteristics. Thus the

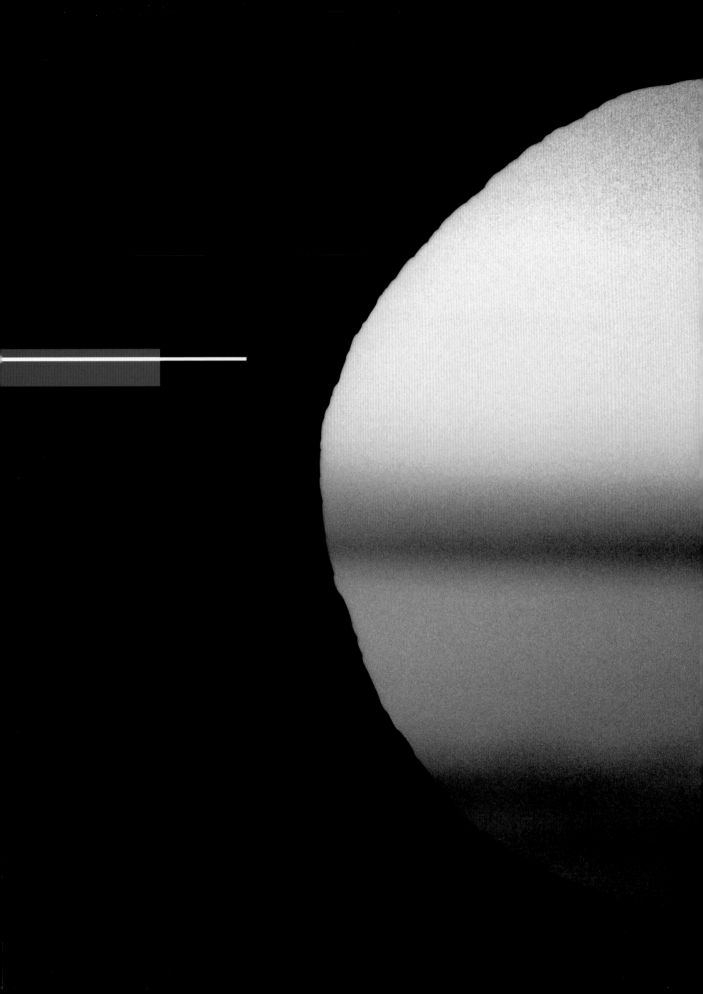

Fire signs – Aries, Leo and Sagittarius – are all enthusiastic, impulsive and energetic; the Earth signs – Taurus, Virgo and Capricorn – are practical and cautious; the Air signs – Gemini, Libra and Aquarius – are thinkers and communicators; the Water signs – Cancer, Scorpio and Pisces – are all romantic and emotional. When we add the signs' zodiacal symbols, the ram, the bull, and so on, to these descriptions, we can begin to build up an even richer picture of each sign's personality.

The symbolism of astrology

There is a logic in astrology's systems of zodiacal rulerships and planetary meanings, but it comes from a former time and once we begin to challenge it, it starts to look very strange, for astrology preserves a way of looking at the world which is no longer generally valued, except perhaps by artists and mystics. It is a symbolic system that brings us close to the world of dreams, one in which ancient myths and legends become part of the fabric of our everyday existence. For example, one idea that we have lost and that influences astrology comes from the ancient Greeks who believed that the universe was alive. The part of the sky that they labelled Leo, for example, actually embodied, or reflected, the same qualities as the lion – courage and regal bearing.

There was also, in the Middle Ages, an entire system of correspondences between planets, zodiac signs and people, animals, stones and herbs. This was known as the Great Chain of Being. Everything, from archangels and human emotions to insects and demons, was linked in a series of vertical and horizontal correspondences. All the signs of the zodiac, for example, were on one horizontal level, while angels, colours, herbs and animals were arranged vertically.

Many of the correspondences seem quite arbitrary nowadays, though sometimes they appear to make sense. For example, it seems natural to relate the Sun to human qualities such as generosity and pride, to kings, to the lion (the king of the jungle), to gold and to sunflowers. Aries, meanwhile, is linked to hot spices through its ruling planet Mars, which itself is considered hot because of its pinkish glow.

When one sees these more obvious connections, it becomes clear that the whole system was based on how we perceive things, how we imagine them to be and the words we use to describe them. This is worlds away from modern science, which tries to tell us how things actually are. Enter the world of astrology and you enter a world of symbolism – adaptable and open to interpretation. What is more, astrological symbols are constantly being reassessed and reinterpreted as the world and society move on.

Astrology, mythology and storytelling

Our earliest myths tell of the lives, loves and passions of the great planetary gods and goddesses, like Venus and Mars, the bringers of passion and war, Mercury the messenger, and Jupiter, the king of the gods. Other stories tell of the 'hero's quest', a theme that was identified by scholars in the nineteenth century. The heroes included figures from Greek legend such as Hercules, Perseus, Theseus and Jason, Gilgamesh from ancient Babylon, or religious figures such as Christ or the Roman god Mithras.

Typically, the hero comes from a mysterious or humble background and is often 'called' to embark on his quest through circumstances beyond his control. That quest consists of challenges such as climbing mountains, navigating oceans, travelling through dark, gloomy forests, encountering demons, fighting off monsters and finally, winning his reward – often a kingdom or a wife.

These tales reveal essential truths about the human condition and about the psychological processes to which we are all subject. They tell, in dramatic form, of the pressures human beings are subjected to on their journey through life – the crises of growing up, going out alone into the world, falling in and out of love, of the challenges of ageing and of the initiations and rites of passage that mark the crucial stages of our lives. Modern psychological astrologers use these ancient, archetypal dramas to provide advice on living, to tell us about ourselves and to help us solve everyday problems. They show us how there is 'no gain without pain', how we have to face up to our inner demons – our fears, phobias, unconscious needs and repressed desires. On the creative level, they can be interpreted as meaning that there can be no art without suffering, that to be truly creative one must first embark on a long, dark journey of the soul. Viewed from this perspective, astrology is, in short, practical mythology, and astrologers may be seen as modern storytellers, the inheritors of an ancient tradition.

But such tales may also be seen as calendar stories, mythical representations of the Sun's annual journey through the heavens – in other words, the passage of the seasons. The period of suffering undergone by the hero represents winter and his eventual triumph indicates the arrival of summer. Thus the world's ancient myths also became the focus of great calendar festivals whose astronomical symbolism was once explicit even though it is now largely forgotten. The ancient Babylonians, for example, celebrated the Akitu – the commemoration of the rescue from the underworld of Marduk, their chief god – at the new moon following the spring equinox. This is the time of year when, in the northern hemisphere, the days become longer than the nights and a new cycle of life and fertility is about to begin. Similarly, the Romans celebrated the rebirth of the Sun god on 25 December, a moment when long nights start to give way to longer days. Christians adopted both these moments of celebration for their own, turning them into the modern festivals of Easter and Christmas respectively and perpetuating our ancestors' fascination with the movement of the stars and planets in the sky.

Each society has its own sequence of festivals, providing a journey through the year in which everybody, young and old, can come together to experience the great seasonal turning points. But this journey through the year, in turn, represents the inner, individual journey we are all on as we go through life. This is a journey that was recognised by the ancient mystics. According to them, the soul enters the body at birth after its passage through the planets. Life's purpose is to prepare for the inevitable return to the stars. Modern astrology, too, sees life as a journey. We pass through the world with our friends and family, but we are all heroes and heroines on our own epic voyage through the stars.

Moon Tables

At a horoscope reading, the astrologer may feel that the sign that the Moon was in at the moment of your birth gives as rich a description of your potential as your Sun sign. Follow the steps below and the tables on the following two pages to find the Moon's position when you were born, then you can also read about your Moon sign.

How to use the tables

N.B. The Moon Tables are based on Greenwich Mean Time at 12 noon and are valid for Europe, Scandinavia and Africa. See Step 7, below, for how to adapt the tables if you were born in a different time zone.

Step 1. Using the tables on pages 18–19 and your birth month and year, note the cycle number (A) and the Moon's zodiac position for the outset of the month (B).

Step 2. Using the cycle number (A) refer to Table 1 (below) and write down the motion.

Step 3. Add your birthdate to the cycle number (A) and write down the resulting motion (again from Table 1).

Step 4. Subtract this from the motion obtained in Step 2 – and you have now found how far the Moon has moved since the start of the month!

Step 5. Add this distance to the original Moon's zodiac position (B). This results in the Moon's position at noon.

Step 6. If you know your birth time, then modify the result from Table 2 opposite.

Step 7. If you were born in the USA or Canada, add 0.1; for India, Pakistan and South-East Asia, subtract 0.1; for Australia, New Zealand and Japan, subtract 0.2.

Step 8. Finally, ignoring figures after the decimal point, refer to Table 3 opposite – this is your Moon sign! If your result is a whole number or nearly a whole number, your Moon sign may be in the adjacent sign, e.g. with a result of 5.9, your Moon sign may actually be in Virgo (6), and similarly with a result of 10.0, it may still be in Sagittarius (9).

Table 1

This table reflects the typical pattern of the Moon's motion, but the starting point will differ from month to month. That information is provided in the tables on pages 18–19.

Cycle	Motion	Cycle	Motion	Cycle	Motion	Cycle	Motion	Cycle	Motion
0	25.5	12	19.8	24	14.9	36	9.4	48	4.2
1	25.1	13	19.4	25	14.5	37	8.9	49	3.8
2	24.6	14	18.9	26	14.1	38	8.5	50	3.4
3	24.2	15	18.5	27	13.6	39	8.0	51	3.0
4	23.7	16	18.1	28	13.2	40	7.5	52	2.6
5	23.2	17	17.7	29	12.8	41	7.1	53	2.2
6	22.7	18	17.3	30	12.3	42	6.6	54	1.8
7	22.2	19	16.9	31	11.8	43	6.2	55	1.3
8	21.7	20	16.5	32	11.4	44	5.8	56	0.9
9	21.3	21	16.1	33	10.9	45	5.4	57	0.4
10	20.8	22	15.7	34	10.4	46	5.0	58	0.0
11	20.3	23	15.3	35	9.9	47	4.6		

Table 2

This table gives the minor changes of the zodiac position during the 24-hour day – so this is for you if you know your time of birth.

Birthtime	Difference
0 to 3 am	- 0.2
4 to 9 am	- 0.1
10 to 2 pm	+ 0.0
3 to 8 pm	+ 0.1
9 to 12 pm	+ 0.2

Table 3

This table takes the result of your calculation and tells you what sign of the zodiac your Moon is in.

Zodiac Sign Numbers			Result
1	13	25	Aries
2	14	26	Taurus
3	15	27	Gemini
4	16	28	Cancer
5	17	29	Leo
6	18	30	Virgo
7	19	31	Libra
8	20	32	Scorpio
9	21	33	Sagittarius
10	22	34	Capricorn
11	23	35	Aquarius
12	24	36	Pisces

Example

for someone born on 27 Feb 2000 at 2am

Step 1.	(A) = 19 (B) = 9.5
Step 2.	Motion for 19 = 16.9
Step 3.	birthdate (27) + cycle number (19) = 46
	Motion = 5.0
Step 4.	16.9 – 5.0 = 11.9
Step 5.	11.9 + 9.5 = 21.4
Step 6.	21.4 – 0.2 = 21.2
Step 7.	optional
Step 8.	21 = **Moon in Sagittarius !!**

	Jan		Feb		Mar		Apr		May		Jun		Jul		Aug		Sep		Oct		Nov		Dec	
	A	B	A	B	A	B	A	B	A	B	A	B	A	B	A	B	A	B	A	B	A	B	A	B
1920	4	1.8	7	3.6	9	4.4	12	6.2	15	7.3	18	8.9	21	10.0	24	11.5	0	1.0	2	2.3	6	4.0	8	5.3
1921	12	7	15	8.6	16	8.9	19	10.4	21	11.4	25	12.9	0	2.0	3	3.7	7	5.5	9	6.8	13	8.5	15	9.6
1922	18	11.2	22	12.6	22	12.9	26	2.4	1	3.6	4	5.3	7	6.6	10	8.4	14	10.1	16	11.2	19	12.7	22	1.8
1923	25	3.2	1	4.8	2	5.1	5	6.8	8	8.1	11	9.9	13	11.1	17	12.7	20	2.1	23	3.2	26	4.7	1	5.9
1924	5	7.6	8	9.3	9	10.2	13	11.9	15	1.0	19	2.6	21	3.6	25	5.1	1	6.7	3	8.0	6	9.7	9.0	11
1925	12	12.7	16	2.3	16	2.6	20	4.0	22	5.1	25	6.6	1	7.7	4	9.4	7	11.2	10	12.5	13	2.2	16	3.3
1926	19	4.8	22	6.3	23	6.6	26	8.1	1	9.3	5	11.1	7	12.4	11	2.1	14	3.8	17	4.9	20	6.3	22	7.4
1927	26	8.9	2	10.5	2	10.8	6	12.5	8	1.8	12	3.6	14	4.8	17	6.3	21	7.8	23	8.9	27	10.4	2	11.6
1928	5	1.3	9	3.1	10	3.9	13	5.6	16	6.7	19	8.2	22	9.3	25	10.8	1	12.4	4	1.7	7	3.5	10	4.7
1929	13	6.4	16	8.0	17	8.2	20	9.7	23	10.7	26	12.2	1	1.4	5	3.1	8	4.9	10	6.2	14	7.9	16	9.0
1930	20	10.5	23	12.0	24	12.3	0	1.8	2	3.0	5	4.8	8	6.1	11	7.8	15	9.4	17	10.5	21	12.0	23	1.1
1931	26	2.6	3	4.2	3	4.5	6	6.2	9	7.5	12	9.3	15	10.4	18	12.0	21	1.5	24	2.5	0	4.1	2	5.3
1932	6	7.1	9	8.8	11	9.6	14	11.3	17	12.4	20	1.9	22	3.0	26	4.5	2	6.1	4	7.4	8	9.2	10	10.4
1933	14	12.1	17	1.6	17	1.9	21	3.3	23	4.4	27	5.9	2	7.1	5	8.8	9	10.6	11	11.9	14	1.5	17	2.7
1934	20	4.2	24	5.7	24	6.0	0	7.5	3	8.7	6	10.5	8	11.8	12	1.5	15	3.1	18	4.2	21	5.7	24	6.7
1935	0	8.2	3	9.9	4	10.2	7	11.9	9	1.2	13	3.0	15	4.1	19	5.7	22	7.1	24	8.2	1	9.8	3	11
1936	6	12.8	10	2.6	11	3.4	15	5.0	17	6.1	21	7.6	23	8.6	26	10.2	2	11.8	5	1.1	8	2.9	11	4.1
1937	14	5.7	18	7.3	18	7.5	21	9.0	24	10.1	0	11.6	2	12.8	6	2.6	9	4.4	12	5.6	15	7.2	17	8.4
1938	21	9.8	24	11.3	25	11.6	1	1.2	3	2.4	7	4.2	9	5.5	13	7.2	16	8.8	18	9.9	22	11.3	24	12.4
1939	0	1.9	4	3.6	4	3.9	8	5.7	10	7.0	13	8.7	16	9.8	19	11.3	23	12.8	25	1.9	1	3.5	4	4.8
1940	7	6.6	10	8.3	12	9.1	15	10.7	18	11.8	21	1.2	24	2.3	0	3.8	3	5.5	5	6.8	9	8.5	11	9.8
1941	15	11.4	18	12.9	19	1.2	22	2.7	24	3.8	1	5.3	3	6.6	6	8.3	10	10.1	12	11.3	16	12.9	18	2.0
1942	21	3.5	25	5.0	25	5.3	1	6.9	4	8.1	7	9.9	10	11.2	13	12.9	17	2.4	19	3.5	22	5.0	25	6.0
1943	1	7.6	4	9.3	5	9.6	8	11.4	11	12.7	14	2.4	16	3.5	20	5.0	23	6.5	26	7.6	2	9.2	4	10.5
1944	8	12.3	11	2.0	12	2.8	16	4.3	18	5.4	22	6.9	24	7.9	0	9.5	4	11.2	6	12.4	10	2.2	12	3.5
1945	15	5.1	19	6.6	19	6.9	23	8.3	25	9.5	1	11.0	4	12.3	7	2.1	10	3.8	13	5.1	16	6.6	19	7.7
1946	22	9.2	26	10.7	26	11.0	2	12.6	4	1.8	8	3.6	10	4.9	14	6.6	17	8.1	20	9.2	23	10.6	25	11.7
1947	2	1.3	5	3.0	5	3.4	9	5.1	11	6.4	15	8.1	17	9.2	20	10.7	24	12.2	26	1.3	2	2.9	5	4.2
1948	8	6	12	7.7	13	8.5	16	10.0	19	11.1	22	12.5	25	1.6	1	3.2	4	4.9	7	6.2	10	7.9	13	9.2
1949	16	10.8	19	12.3	20	12.5	23	2.0	26	3.1	2	4.8	4	6.0	8	7.8	11	9.6	13	10.8	17	12.3	19	1.4
1950	23	2.8	26	4.4	27	4.6	3	6.3	5	7.5	8	9.3	11	10.6	14	12.2	18	1.8	20	2.8	24	4.3	26	5.4
1951	2	7	6	8.7	6	9.1	9	10.9	12	12.1	15	1.8	18	2.9	21	4.4	24	5.8	0	7.0	3	8.7	5	9.9
1952	9	11.7	12	1.4	14	2.1	17	3.7	20	4.7	23	6.2	25	7.3	1	8.9	5	10.6	7	11.9	11	1.6	13	2.9
1953	17	44	20	5.9	20	6.2	24	7.7	26	8.8	2	10.5	5	11.8	8	1.5	12	3.3	14	4.5	17	6.0	20	7.0
1954	23	8.5	27	10.0	0	10.3	3	11.9	6	1.2	9	3.0	12	4.3	15	5.9	18	7.4	21	8.5	24	10.0	27	11.1
1955	3	12.7	6	2.5	7	2.9	10	4.6	12	5.9	16	7.4	18	8.5	22	10.0	25	11.5	0	12.7	4	2.4	6	3.6
1956	9	5.4	13	7.1	14	7.8	18	9.3	20	10.4	24	11.8	26	13.0	2	2.6	5	4.3	8	5.6	11	7.3	14	8.6
1957	17	10.1	21	11.6	21	11.9	24	1.4	0	2.5	3	4.2	5	5.5	9	7.3	12	9.0	15	10.1	18	11.6	20	12.7
1958	24	2.2	0	3.7	0	4.0	4	5.6	6	6.9	10	8.7	12	10.0	16	11.6	19	1.1	21	2.2	25	3.7	0	4.8
1959	3	6.5	7	8.2	7	8.6	11	10.3	13	11.6	16	1.1	19	2.2	22	3.7	26	5.2	1	6.3	4	8.0	7	9.3
1960	10	11.1	13	12.8	15	1.5	18	3.0	21	4.0	24	5.5	27	6.6	3	8.3	6	10.0	9	11.3	12	1.1	14	2.2
1961	18	3.8	21	5.3	22	5.6	25	7.1	0	8.2	4	9.9	6	11.2	9	13.0	13	2.7	15	3.8	19	5.3	21	6.4
1962	25	7.8	1	9.4	1	9.7	4	11.3	7	12.6	10	2.4	13	3.7	16	5.3	20	6.8	22	7.8	25	9.4	0	10.5
1963	4	12.2	7	2.0	8	2.3	11	4.1	14	5.3	17	6.8	19	7.9	23	9.3	26	10.8	1	12.0	5	1.7	7	3.0
1964	11	4.8	14	6.4	15	7.1	19	8.6	21	9.7	25	11.2	0	12.3	3	2.0	7	3.8	9	5.1	13	6.8	15	8.0
1965	18	9.5	22	10.9	22	11.2	26	12.7	1	1.9	4	3.6	7	4.9	10	6.7	13	8.4	16	9.5	19	11.0	22	12
1966	25	1.5	1	3.0	2	3.3	5	5.1	7	6.4	11	8.1	13	9.4	17	10.9	20	12.4	23	1.5	26	3.0	1	4.2
1967	5	5.9	8	7.7	8	8.1	12	9.8	14	10.9	18	12.5	20	1.5	23	3.0	0	4.5	2	5.7	5	7.4	8	8.7
1968	11	10.5	15	12.1	16	12.8	20	2.3	22	3.4	25	4.9	0	6.0	4	7.7	7	9.5	10	10.8	13	12.5	16	1.6
1969	19	3.1	22	4.6	23	4.9	26	6.4	1	7.6	5	9.3	7	10.6	11	12.4	14	2.0	16	3.1	20	4.6	22	5.7

	Jan		Feb		Mar		Apr		May		Jun		Jul		Aug		Sep		Oct		Nov		Dec	
	A	B	A	B	A	B	A	B	A	B	A	B	A	B	A	B	A	B	A	B	A	B	A	B
970	26	7.1	2	8.7	2	9.1	6	10.8	8	12.1	12	1.8	14	3.1	17	4.6	21	6.1	23	7.2	27	8.7	2	9.9
971	5	11.7	9	1.5	9	1.8	12	3.5	15	4.6	18	6.1	21	7.2	24	8.6	0	10.2	3	11.4	6	1.1	8	2.4
972	12	4.2	15	5.8	17	6.5	20	8.0	23	9.1	26	10.6	1	11.8	4	1.5	8	3.3	10	4.5	14	6.2	16	7.3
973	20	8.8	23	10.3	23	10.5	0	12.1	2	1.3	5	3.0	8	4.3	11	6.0	15	7.7	17	8.8	20	10.3	23	11.3
974	26	12.8	2	2.4	3	2.8	6	4.5	9	5.8	12	7.6	15	8.8	18	10.3	21	11.8	24	12.9	0	2.4	2	3.6
975	6	5.4	9	7.2	10	7.5	13	9.1	15	10.3	19	11.8	21	12.8	25	2.3	1	3.9	3	5.1	7	6.8	9	8.1
976	12	9.8	16	11.4	17	12.2	21	1.6	23	2.7	27	4.3	2	5.5	5	7.2	9	9.0	11	10.3	14	11.9	17	1.0
977	20	2.5	24	3.9	24	4.2	0	5.7	3	6.9	6	8.7	8	10.0	12	11.7	15	1.4	18	2.5	21	3.9	24	5.0
978	0	6.5	3	8.2	3	8.5	7	10.3	9	11.6	13	1.3	15	2.5	19	4.0	22	5.5	24	6.5	0	8.1	3	9.3
979	6	11.1	10	12.9	10	1.1	14	2.8	16	3.9	19	5.4	22	6.5	25	8.0	1	9.6	4	10.8	7	12.6	10	1.8
980	13	3.6	16	5.1	18	5.8	21	7.3	24	8.4	0	10.0	2	11.2	6	12.9	9	2.7	12	4.0	15	5.6	17	6.7
981	21	8.1	24	9.6	25	9.9	1	11.4	3	12.6	7	2.4	9	3.7	12	5.4	16	7.0	18	8.1	22	9.6	24	10.7
982	0	12.2	4	1.9	4	2.3	7	4.0	10	5.3	13	7.0	16	8.2	19	9.6	23	11.1	25	12.2	1	1.8	4	3.0
983	7	4.8	10	6.6	11	6.8	14	8.5	17	9.6	20	11.1	22	12.2	26	1.7	2	3.3	4	4.5	8	6.3	10	7.6
984	14	9.3	17	10.8	19	11.5	22	13.0	24	2.1	0	3.7	3	4.9	6	6.7	10	8.5	12	9.7	16	11.3	18	12.3
985	21	1.8	25	3.3	25	3.5	1	5.1	4	6.3	7	8.1	10	9.4	13	11.1	16	12.7	19	1.8	22	3.3	25	4.4
986	1	6	4	7.6	5	8.0	8	9.8	11	11.1	14	12.7	16	1.8	20	3.3	23	4.8	26	5.9	2	7.5	4	8.7
987	8	10.5	11	12.3	11	12.5	15	2.1	17	3.3	21	4.7	23	5.8	26	7.3	3	9.0	5	10.3	8	12.0	11	1.3
988	14	3	18	4.5	19	5.2	23	6.7	25	7.8	1	9.4	3	10.6	7	12.4	10	2.2	13	3.4	16	4.9	19	6.0
989	22	7.4	25	8.9	26	9.2	2	10.8	4	12.0	8	1.8	10	3.1	14	4.8	17	6.4	19	7.5	23	8.9	25	10.1
990	1	11.7	5	1.4	5	1.7	9	3.5	11	4.8	15	6.4	17	7.5	20	9.0	24	10.4	26	11.5	2	1.2	5	2.4
991	8	4.2	12	5.9	12	6.2	15	7.8	18	8.9	21	10.4	24	11.5	0	1.0	3	2.7	6	4.0	9	5.8	11	7.0
992	15	8.7	18	10.2	20	10.9	23	12.3	26	1.4	2	3.1	4	4.3	8	6.1	11	7.8	13	9.0	17	10.6	19	11.6
993	23	1.1	26	2.6	26	2.9	3	4.5	5	5.8	8	7.6	11	8.8	14	10.5	18	12.0	20	1.1	23	2.6	26	3.7
994	2	5.4	5	7.1	6	7.5	9	9.2	12	10.5	15	12.1	18	1.2	21	2.6	24	4.1	27	5.2	3	6.8	5	8.1
995	9	9.9	12	11.6	13	11.9	16	1.5	18	2.6	22	4.1	24	5.2	0	6.8	4	8.4	6	9.7	10	11.5	12	12.8
996	15	2.4	19	3.8	20	4.5	24	6.0	26	7.1	2	8.7	5	10.0	8	11.8	12	1.5	14	2.7	17	4.2	20	5.3
997	23	6.8	27	8.3	0	8.6	3	10.2	6	11.5	9	1.3	11	2.6	15	4.2	18	5.7	21	6.8	24	8.3	27	9.4
998	3	11.1	6	12.9	6	1.2	10	2.9	12	4.2	16	5.7	18	6.8	22	8.3	25	9.7	0	10.9	4	12.5	6	1.8
999	9	3.6	13	5.3	13	5.6	17	7.2	19	8.3	22	9.8	25	10.9	1	12.5	4	2.2	7	3.5	10	5.3	13	6.5
000	16	8	19	9.5	21	10.2	24	11.6	27	12.8	3	2.4	5	3.7	9	5.5	12	7.2	15	8.4	18	9.9	20	11.0
001	24	12.4	0	2.0	0	2.3	4	4.0	6	5.2	10	7.0	12	8.3	15	9.9	19	11.4	21	12.5	25	2.0	0	3.1
002	3	4.8	7	6.6	7	6.9	10	8.6	13	9.8	16	11.4	19	12.5	22	1.9	26	3.4	1	4.6	4	6.2	7	7.5
003	10	9.3	13	11.0	14	11.3	17	12.9	20	2.0	23	3.4	25	4.6	2	6.2	5	7.9	7	9.2	11	11.0	13	12.2
004	17	1.7	20	3.2	22	3.8	25	5.3	0	6.4	3	8.1	6	9.4	9	11.2	13	12.9	15	2.0	19	3.6	21	4.6
005	24	6.1	1	7.7	1	8.0	4	9.7	7	11.0	10	12.8	13	2.0	16	3.6	19	5.1	22	6.2	25	7.7	0	8.8
006	4	10.5	7	12.3	8	12.6	11	2.3	14	3.5	17	5.1	19	6.1	23	7.6	26	9.1	1	10.3	5	12.0	7	1.2
007	11	3	14	4.7	14	5.0	18	6.5	20	7.6	24	9.1	26	10.2	2	11.9	6	1.6	8	2.9	11	4.7	14	5.9
008	17	7.4	21	8.8	22	9.5	26	11.0	1	12.1	4	1.8	7	3.1	10	4.9	13	6.6	16	7.7	19	9.2	22	10.3
009	25	11.8	1	1.4	2	1.7	5	3.4	7	4.7	11	6.5	13	7.7	17	9.3	20	10.7	22	11.8	26	1.3	1	2.5
010	4	4.2	8	6.0	8	6.2	12	8.0	14	9.2	18	10.7	20	11.8	23	1.3	27	2.8	2	4.0	5	5.7	8	7.0
011	11	8.7	15	10.4	15	10.7	18	12.2	21	1.3	24	2.8	27	3.9	3	5.6	6	7.4	9	8.7	12	10.4	14	11.5
012	18	1	21	2.5	23	3.1	26	4.6	1	5.8	5	7.5	7	8.8	11	10.6	14	12.2	16	1.4	20	2.9	22	4.0
013	26	5.5	2	7.1	2	7.4	6	9.2	8	10.5	11	12.2	14	1.4	17	2.9	21	4.4	23	5.5	27	7.0	2	8.2
014	5	9.9	8	11.7	9	11.9	12	1.7	15	2.8	18	4.4	21	5.5	24	6.9	0	8.5	3	9.7	6	11.4	8	12.7
015	12	2.5	15	4.1	16	4.4	19	5.9	21	7.0	25	8.5	0	9.6	3	11.3	7	1.1	9	2.4	13	4.1	15	5.2
016	18	6.7	22	8.1	23	8.8	27	10.3	2	11.5	5	1.2	8	2.5	11	4.3	15	5.9	17	7.1	20	8.6	23	9.7
017	26	11.2	2	12.8	3	1.1	6	2.9	9	4.2	12	5.9	14	7.1	18	8.6	21	10.1	24	11.1	0	12.7	2	1.8
018	6	3.6	9	5.4	9	5.6	13	7.3	15	8.5	19	10.0	21	11.1	25	12.6	1	2.2	3	3.4	7	5.2	9	6.5
019	12	8.2	16	9.8	16	10.1	20	11.6	22	12.6	25	2.1	1	3.3	4	5.0	7	6.8	10	8.0	13	9.7	16	10.9

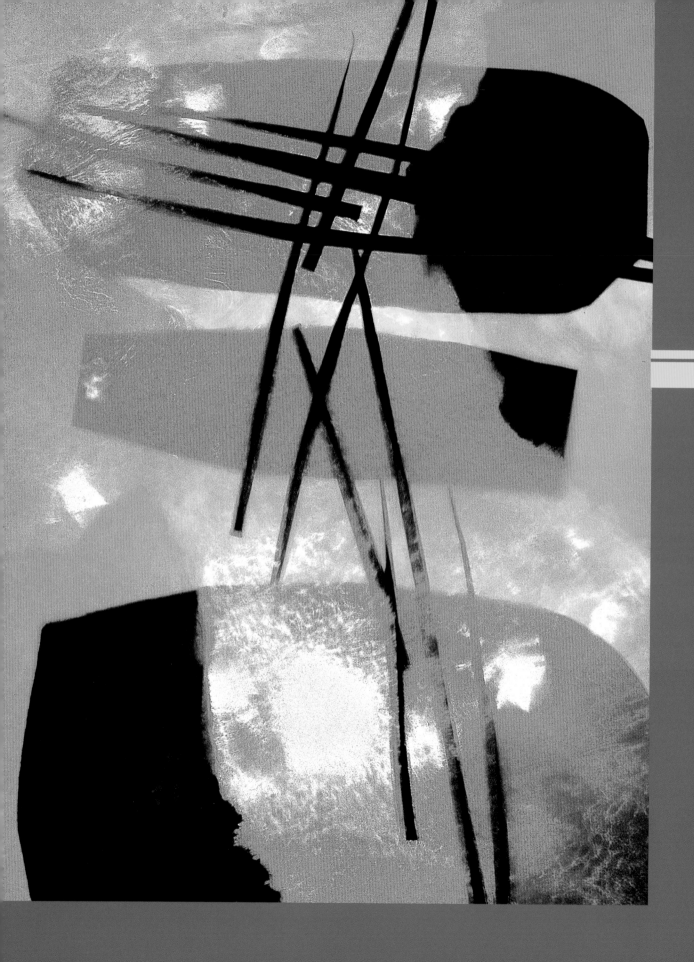

aries

cardinal, fire, male

21 march – 20 april

ON 21 MARCH, LIGHT AND DARK ARE PERFECTLY BALANCED, DAY AND NIGHT ARE EQUAL LENGTHS, POISED ON THE BRINK OF A NEW CYCLE. THE WORLD IS COILED LIKE A SPRING, READY TO UNWIND. ARIES IS THE LEADER, THE VERY FIRST SIGN OF THE ZODIAC, THE SYMBOL OF UNLIMITED POWER AND INDIVIDUALITY. IT IS A SIGN OF FRESH STARTS AND NEW BEGINNINGS, OF ENTERPRISE AND ENERGY. ARIES' STRENGTH IS ITS WILLINGNESS TO TAKE RISKS AND GIVE ORDERS. ITS VIRTUES ARE ITS HONESTY AND SHEER ENTHUSIASM, AND ITS ABILITY TO INSPIRE THE OTHER ELEVEN SIGNS WITH ITS FIERY AND POWERFUL EXAMPLE.

THE PAWNEE PEOPLE OF NORTH AMERICA
CALLED MARS — ARIES' RULING PLANET — GREAT STAR AND
PORTRAYED HIM AS A FIERCE, RED-PAINTED WARRIOR. GREAT STAR WISHED
TO MARRY BRIGHT STAR (VENUS), BUT TO DETER HIM, SHE SET HIM TEN IMPOSSIBLE
CHALLENGES. NEEDLESS TO SAY, HE EVENTUALLY WON HIS BRIDE AND ONCE THE TWO
WERE UNITED, HUMANITY AND ALL THE GOODNESS OF THE WORLD WERE CREATED.

THE GREEK LEGEND OF JASON AND THE GOLDEN FLEECE IS ALSO AN ARIES MYTH. IN IT, JASON ASKED
HIS UNCLE PELIAS FOR HIS RIGHTFUL HALF OF THE KINGDOM OF THESSALY. PELIAS SAID HE WOULD
HAND IT OVER, BUT ON CONDITION: THAT JASON BRING HIM THE FLEECE OF A CERTAIN GOLDEN RAM
THAT COULD FLY AND HAD THE POWERS OF REASON AND SPEECH. THE FLEECE WAS OWNED BY AETES OF
COLCHIS, WHERE IT HUNG FROM A TREE GUARDED BY A VICIOUS DRAGON. JASON SAILED TO COLCHIS
WITH HIS COMPANIONS, THE ARGONAUTS. IN COLCHIS AETES AGREED TO GIVE HIM THE FLEECE BUT
SET HIM A SERIES OF CHALLENGES. LUCKILY FOR JASON, AETES' DAUGHTER MEDEA FELL IN LOVE
WITH HIM AND USED HER MAGIC TO HELP HIM. JASON AND MEDEA
MARRIED AND WERE HAPPY UNTIL JASON LEFT MEDEA
FOR ANOTHER WOMAN. MEDEA'S REVENGE
WAS CRUEL. SHE MURDERED HER
CHILDREN AND JASON'S
NEW BRIDE.

THE
PAWNEE STORY IS A CREATION
STORY BUT ALSO SHOWS ARIES' ENERGY AND
RESOURCEFULNESS. ALTHOUGH JASON IS A STRONG
AND BRAVE LEADER, HIS STORY DEMONSTRATES THAT,
HOWEVER COURAGEOUS WE MAY BE, WE CANNOT ALWAYS
ACHIEVE SUCCESS ON OUR OWN. HIS MISFORTUNE IS ALSO
A WARNING NOT TO RIDE ROUGHSHOD OVER OTHERS.
WE ALL — BUT ARIES IN PARTICULAR — NEED TO
RECOGNISE THAT OTHER PEOPLE HAVE FEELINGS
AND THAT THEY MAY BE HURT BY OUR
WORDS OR ACTIONS.

individual
in the lead
assertive
aggressive
commanding
confrontational
conquering
positive
pro-active

red, iron, ruby

Aries kick-starts the entire chain of cosmic existence, so, as one might expect, it is the sign of rebirth and new beginnings. As a Cardinal sign governed by Mars and the first of the Fire signs, Aries represents creativity, enthusiasm and initiative. It is also the strongest, toughest sign in the zodiac, full of drive and ambition and, not surprisingly, frequently impatient of others. After all, someone who sees themself as a visionary often wishes to press ahead as fast as possible and may resent those who stand in their way or move more slowly.

So much verve and purpose can also make Ariens people of extremes. Seized by a sudden urge or fresh idea, they can go shooting off in almost any direction, putting all their energy into their new-found enterprise. In the world of work, Aries should take care to choose a profession that gives scope to its aspirations and leadership skills, for if it is stuck in a dull, routine job, frustration can build up and manifest itself as depression.

Because Aries is such a go-getter, it often finds it hard to deal with failure. A lesson it needs to learn is to give itself permission to fail. It might help if it tried to accept that if its plans do not work out, this might be to its advantage. Perhaps it is being saved for something better. In the event of failure, a good Arien strategy is to watch out for new opportunities and make a fresh start as quickly as possible. Perhaps it should try a different approach or a novel area of endeavour. Being Aries, sooner or later it will find another route to success.

The ambitious, driven side of Aries' nature means that it may be accused of arrogance, intolerance, prickliness and overbearing behaviour. Ambition may also lead to selfishness and this can be another dark side of the Aries personality. And Aries' headstrong nature – symbolised by the ram – also can result in its speaking without

mars

MOST OF ARIES' ASSOCIATIONS COME THROUGH
ITS RULING PLANET, MARS. WITH ITS REDDISH HUE,
THIS PLANET WAS SEEN BY ANCIENT ASTROLOGERS AS BEING
HOT, AGGRESSIVE AND WAR-LIKE — AFTER ALL, MARS IS THE
GOD OF WAR. IT IS NO SURPRISE THEN THAT ARIES HAS THE
REPUTATION FOR BEING FIERCE AND ASSERTIVE — A REAL
GO-GETTER WHO LETS NOTHING STAND IN ITS WAY. THE
PSYCHOLOGIST CARL JUNG SAW THE MYTHICAL MARS AS
REPRESENTING THE MALE SIDE OF PEOPLE'S PERSONALITIES
— SOMETHING WE ALL POSSESS WHETHER
WE ARE MALE OR FEMALE.

thinking or acting without considering the consequences – again with problematic results for all concerned. Notable people born with the Sun in Aries include Bismarck – Germany's 'Iron Chancellor' – Vincent van Gogh, Diana Ross, Hans Christian Andersen, Bette Davies, Alec Guinness, Harry Houdini, Henry James, Thomas Jefferson and Charlie Chaplin.

Aries' relationships

People who are happy handing over responsibility to others may well be attracted to Aries' powers of leadership. They can sit back while Aries gives the orders, makes up their minds for them and releases them from the need to take any decisions of their own. As a result, Aries can find itself being overwhelmed as it takes on increasingly more responsibility.

Another problem for Aries is that it sometimes has a very simple, straightforward view of the world and as a result sometimes forms one-sided impressions of people. This means that it often idealises its partners, placing enormous pressure on them. When two people worship one another they can live in this world of illusion for a while, but you do not have to be a genius to work out that once Aries discovers that its partner is only human, it will not be long before it is disappointed. Aries badly needs to remember that loved ones have feet of clay. It must learn to acknowledge – and love – its partner's weaknesses as well as his or her strengths.

In many relationships, the preservation of peace and harmony is crucial, but this simple truth can take Aries a long time to learn. Its easiest relationships are often with the other Fire signs. Aries and Leo have in common an

the ram

Aries' creature is the ram, an animal known for its daring, headstrong qualities, so Ariens are often regarded as the sort of people who rush in where others fear to tread. Perhaps that is why in myths and fairy tales, Aries is personified by ambitious, superhuman heroes and heroines who fearlessly embark on great quests to vanquish evil and win honour, fame and fortune.

ability to make sweeping changes in their lives, while Aries and Sagittarius share an adventurous spirit and a willingness to take risks. If two Fire signs both demand the limelight – something that can be particularly evident in a relationship between two Ariens – there can be problems. So what can be done? The first step is for each to let the other be the centre of attention from time to time and to accept that the other's priorities can be as valid as one's own.

The classic Arien relationship is with Libra – an Air sign. Based on the assumption that opposites attract, Aries finds refuge in Libra's soothing arms, the gentle surroundings it creates and its graceful lifestyle. Libra, meanwhile, is often mightily impressed by Aries' sheer energy and belief in itself. But if the signs fall out, Libra can be alienated by what it sees as Aries' unrelenting bossiness, while Aries begins to despise what it views as Libra's lack of willpower and its inability to make up its mind. Relationships with the other two Air signs, Gemini and Aquarius, tend to be lively. At their best, Geminian and Aquarian ideas combine with Arien enthusiasm to form an explosive mixture. Yet instant attraction can burn itself out unless each partner is dedicated to making the association work.

Aries' relationships with the three Earth signs – Taurus, Virgo and Capricorn – are sometimes not the easiest, mainly because Earth's natural caution clashes with Aries' risk-taking. Yet Taurus may provide the stability that

life-enhancing strategies

- REMEMBER THE DIFFERENCE BETWEEN BEING ASSERTIVE (STANDING UP FOR YOURSELF) AND BEING AGGRESSIVE (PUSHING PEOPLE AROUND).

- IS THERE SOMEONE YOU HAVE OFFENDED RECENTLY, EVEN WITHOUT MEANING TO? PHONE THEM OR WRITE THEM A LETTER. ASK IF THEY ARE FEELING ALL RIGHT AND APOLOGISE SINCERELY FOR YOUR BEHAVIOUR.

- BE CONSCIOUS OF HOW YOUR WORDS AND ACTIONS CAN AFFECT OTHERS. TRY NOT TO LET THEM FEEL PUSHED AROUND AND MAKE SURE THEY SEE YOU ARE REALLY LISTENING TO THEM.

- SLOW DOWN AND WAIT FOR OTHER PEOPLE TO CATCH UP WITH YOUR THOUGHTS AND ACTIONS AND ENCOURAGE THEM TO TAKE ON MORE RESPONSIBILITY FOR THEMSELVES. IN THIS WAY, YOU WILL NOT FEEL OVER-BURDENED AND THEY WILL LEARN THAT THEY CANNOT RELY ON YOU FOR EVERYTHING IN LIFE.

- RESPECT THE RIGHT OF OTHERS TO THEIR OWN NEEDS AND OPINIONS RATHER THAN EXPECTING THEM TO WANT AND BELIEVE THE SAME THINGS AS YOU.

- IF YOU ARE A PARENT, OFFER PATIENT ENCOURAGEMENT TO YOUR CHILD INSTEAD OF REACHING INSTANT JUDGEMENTS ABOUT WHETHER WHAT HE OR SHE IS DOING IS RIGHT OR WRONG.

- AND ABOVE ALL, IF EVERYONE AROUND YOU IS REFUSING TO TAKE THE LEAD, THEN YOU MUST!

Aries lacks, while Aries may inject a shot of energy and ambition into Taurus's stable lifestyle. Virgo benefits from the vitality Aries brings to the relationship. In return, Aries' impulsiveness is smoothed out with Virgo's efficiency and organisational skills. Capricorn lends Aries its common sense and business skills, but the two signs can clash if both try to control the home environment: a little give and take is advised!

Aries' relationships with the three Water signs – Cancer, Scorpio and Pisces – bring a different picture. These three are emotional and sensitive, so can make Aries feel truly adored while, for its part, Aries can make Water aware of feelings it never knew it had. But Water can be wounded by Aries' insensitivity and Aries can get fed up with Water's apparent lack of initiative. Aries and Cancer often clash because each believes that it was born to give the orders. With Aries and Scorpio there may be a falling out if Scorpio fails to say what it feels and if Aries takes Scorpio's loyalty for granted. Aries and Pisces, meanwhile, drift apart when Aries wants everything to be done its way. Pisces will not argue with that – it will simply go off into its own world.

On the whole, a relationship with an Aries person succeeds when the differences between the two people are valued as much as the similarities. Ariens can help their loved ones by boosting their confidence, praising and

flattering them. It is a matter of giving love, not asking for it. Being people of extremes, Ariens can make heavy demands on others, but they also can give so much love that their partners feel suffocated. And while Aries can often prove to be a firm friend, because it hates to lose a battle, it can also be a worst enemy – not someone to cross if you can possibly avoid it!

But although Aries mostly needs to temper its wild unrestrained energy with a measure of tact and diplomacy, it should occasionally let rip and behave unreasonably. There will be plenty of time for being cool, calm and collected – like a good Libran – once the emotional storm has passed.

Aries' health and wellbeing

In medical astrology, Aries rules the head, so the ailments that Aries typically suffers from include headaches and migraines, and problems with the ears, nose and mouth. Aries may also have health problems arising from its headstrong, accident-inducing, rash behaviour, its tendency to overwork and take risks and the stress that all these activities can induce.

Red wine and chocolate – both of which are stimulants and so are traditionally associated with the sign of Aries – are sometimes known to trigger migraines, but we do not always understand the causes of the more everyday sort of headaches. Nevertheless, it seems that many are stress-induced, so it follows that, to avoid recurrent headaches, Aries individuals would do well to take simple stress-reducing precautions. A first step, for example, might be to emulate Libra – Aries' opposite sign – and aim for a balanced lifestyle, matching work with

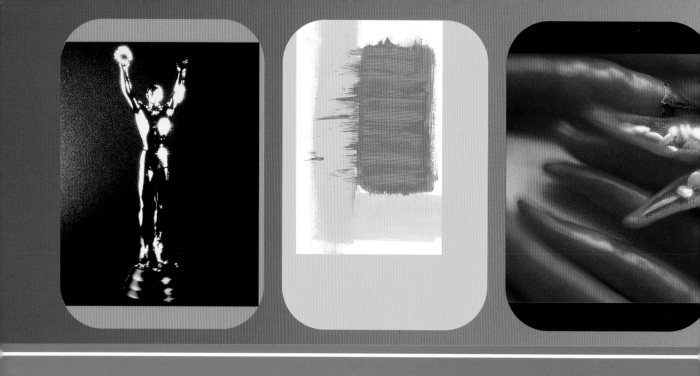

relaxation, intellectual activity with physical exercise. As we now know, even half-an-hour's exercise a day can go a long way towards reducing levels of stress.

But which exercise to choose? The typical Aries person is often in a hurry, so an activity such as running or jogging might seem ideal. But in fact, Aries needs to learn to slow down, so it would do better to take up gentle walking, enjoying the scenery and taking in the view as he or she goes along.

Competitive sports are another exercise option for success-oriented Ariens, for they often revel in the opportunity to be a winner. But inevitably, Aries is not always content with being a team player. It would be happier in a leadership role such as team captain or coach. And if, during a match, Aries gets stressed-out by what it sees as other players' incompetence – real or imagined – the worst he or she can do is indulge in a bout of head-banging confrontation. That is when stress can really kick in. Instead, a spell in the gym knocking the stuffing out of a punch bag is a healthy way to work off pent-up anger. And if Aries has been rude to another player, he or she should offer a calm and sincere apology – however difficult that might be.

Being an energetic sign, Aries rules caffeine-rich stimulants such as tea and coffee. There is nothing wrong with a little indulgence in these, although addicts – whether born under the sign of Aries or not – should try doing without caffeine and instead allow their natural energy to keep them going. In that way they can avoid the classic late-afternoon crash, when sugar-levels drop and weariness takes over. If you recognise that you have become addicted to caffeine, it is important, though, to wean yourself off it slowly.

Because they are in a constant hurry, Aries people also tend to eat too fast, and this is a habit that often generates indigestion. The obvious solution for anyone who does this is to chew food carefully and slowly.

Aries feels happiest in clean, light, uncluttered environments. If there is too much mess around, he or she may feel depressed, hemmed in or tied down. It is as if the mess symbolises the crushing weight of responsibilities that accumulate during the course of one's life. To restore its equilibrium and preserve its independence and sense of freedom, Aries might like to sweep through his or her house or apartment, disposing of anything that is not essential. Such a clean-out not only helps to create the ordered environment Aries prefers, but also provides a sort of spiritual spring-clean. And if Aries is troubled by the sense that it is living amidst fussily coloured, busy décor, it could take the more drastic step of redecorating using simple, bold colours or pure white. With a blank canvas like this as a background, the stage is set for Aries to make a truly fresh start.

festivals

Although in the modern Western calendar we begin the year in January, just after midwinter, many societies, such as that of ancient Babylon, started theirs with the spring equinox. Astrologers also begin the wheel of the zodiac at the spring equinox, the moment at which day and night are exactly the same length. This moment in time is known to astronomers as the 'first point of Aries'. Although the idea of the year starting with the spring equinox has now largely been lost, a relic of it remains in the way in which, in many countries, the financial year begins and ends in April.

But the spring equinox is far more than a moment to finalise business accounts. In many religions it is an event of profound religious significance, symbolising renewal, liberation from darkness to light, or death followed by resurrection – all Arien themes studied at the end of the nineteenth century by the writer James Frazer. In his book *The Golden Bough*, Frazer concluded that the motif of the dying god that occurs in religions across the world is part of the same story, celebrating both the rebirth of the sun and the start of a new cycle in nature.

The Jewish festival of Passover is one such rebirth story. It begins at the full moon following the spring equinox and commemorates the exodus of the Jews from slavery in Egypt. The Jews' new-found freedom can be interpreted not only as a physical rebirth but also as a spiritual one.

The Akitu was a twelve-day spring equinox festival celebrated in the days of the ancient Babylonians. First came four days of purification, followed by a day of atonement when the population mourned the death of its chief

take a leaf from aries

THE CELEBRATION OF BOTH PASSOVER AND EASTER INCLUDE THE COMMUNAL BREAKING OF BREAD AND DRINKING OF WINE, SYMBOLISING THE BOND OF FRIENDSHIP THAT RESULTS WHEN FOOD IS SHARED. CELEBRATE THE SPRING EQUINOX AND WITH IT THE ARRIVAL OF A NEW CYCLE OF GROWTH BY PREPARING A MEAL FOR FAMILY AND FRIENDS, USING FRESH INGREDIENTS — PERHAPS FOOD YOU HAVE GROWN YOURSELF. DECORATE YOUR HOME WITH FLOWERS TO WELCOME IN THE NEW YEAR.

god, Marduk. Next came three days of wild commotion in the streets while the people 'searched' high and low for their god. At the end of this, Marduk was 'rescued from the underworld', an event that was followed by public celebration, with the statues of the gods carried in procession and the oracles consulted to see what might be in store for the people during the coming year. Such was the importance of the Akitu that devout Babylonians believed that at times when Babylon was occupied by its enemies – as for instance when they were overcome by the Assyrians – this was the result of the people's failure to celebrate the festival regularly. According to them, the gods, in their anger, had abandoned the Babylonians to their fate.

It is immediately apparent that the mythical patterns of the more ancient celebrations of Passover and the Akitu underpin the observance of Easter – the commemoration of Christ's crucifixion on Good Friday and His resurrection on Easter Sunday. The idea of fertility and of Nature's endless cycle is actually embodied in the word 'Easter', which comes from the name of the Teutonic goddess, Eostre, whose name also gives us the word 'oestrogen' – the female hormone. In fact, eggs as a symbol of fertility and of the cycle of life often play their part in spring equinox stories. It was customary, for example, to organise egg hunts in honour of Eostre: one person hid a number of eggs and everyone else searched for them. The giving of chocolate eggs to children at Easter is the most popular legacy of this ancient pagan practice, while the traditional Passover meal includes hard-boiled eggs as a symbol of rebirth and the renewal and continuity of life.

aries teaches us all to be courageous and energetic,

a meditation

THIS MEDITATION HELPS ARIES TO REMOVE TIES TO THE PAST WHICH CAN GET IN THE WAY OF THOSE ALL-IMPORTANT ARIEN FRESH STARTS. THE INDIAN TEACHER BAGWAN SRI RAJNEESH BELIEVED THAT WESTERNERS COULD NOT STAY STILL LONG ENOUGH TO MEDITATE PROPERLY. THIS IS OFTEN AN ARIES PROBLEM, BUT IT IS SHARED BY MANY WHO WERE NOT BORN IN THIS SIGN. SO, IF IT HELPS TO MOVE, FEEL FREE TO DO SO.

Close your eyes and concentrate on breathing slowly and deeply. Imagine that you are surrounded by a white light and complete emptiness. One by one, imagine your possessions, commitments and relationships. How does each one feel? Does it have a colour, a shape, a smell? Does it tie you to the past? Does it support you or make you feel trapped? Slowly, when you are ready, change the images you associate with each – its appearance, colour, sound or other sensations. As you do this, you should begin to get a feeling of control. Then, if you wish, you can completely remove the images from your mind until all that remains is the bright, white emptiness. When you are ready, open your eyes. You will feel more positive about your ability to make improvements to your life. You will no longer have a sense of being held back by past choices you have made or by old circumstances that surround you.

constellation

FOR SUCH AN IMPORTANT SIGN, THE CONSTELLATION OF ARIES IS ONE OF THE SMALLEST. ITS STARS ARE DIFFICULT TO SPOT EXCEPT BY REFERENCE TO ITS LARGER NEIGHBOUR, THE CONSTELLATION OF PISCES, AND THEY ARE WELL-NIGH IMPOSSIBLE TO SEE WHEN CITY LIGHTS OBSCURE THE NIGHT SKY. SOME THINK THAT ARIES WAS ONE OF THE LAST CONSTELLATIONS TO BE CREATED, SO THERE WAS NOT MUCH SPACE LEFT IN THE HEAVENS, BUT OTHERS SEE SYMBOLISM IN THE FACT THAT IT IS SO HARD TO FIND. THEY SEE ARIES AS A CONSTELLATION THAT EMERGES OUT OF NOTHING, JUST AS AT THE SPRING EQUINOX THE UNIVERSE ONCE AGAIN GIVES BIRTH TO ITSELF, AND LIGHT EMERGES FROM THE DARKNESS OF WINTER.

to take the lead and initiate new enterprises

taurus

fixed, earth, female

21 april – 21 may

IN TAURUS, THE SOLAR JOURNEY ENTERS A PHASE OF FERTILITY AND THE INITIATIVES SET IN TRAIN IN ARIES START TO TAKE ROOT AND DEVELOP. TAURUS IS A SIGN OF THE LOYALTY THAT UNITES TWO PEOPLE FOR LIFE. IT IS ALSO CONNECTED TO MATERIAL POSSESSIONS AND PHYSICAL PLEASURE. PEOPLE BORN UNDER TAURUS ARE SOMETIMES LET DOWN BY THEIR OBSTINACY AND THEIR REFUSAL TO TAKE RISKS. YET THEIR STRENGTHS ARE THEIR GREAT DETERMINATION TO STICK TO A COURSE OF ACTION THROUGH ANY ADVERSITY AND THEIR ABILITY TO PRESERVE THE BEST OF THE PAST.

TAUREAN MYTHS ARE FULL OF STORIES CONCERNING BULLS. THE ANCIENT BABYLONIAN BULL OF HEAVEN WAS A DESTRUCTIVE BEAST CREATED BY ANU, THE GOD OF THE SKY, FOR HIS DAUGHTER, ISHTAR. IT WAS OVERCOME BY KING GILGAMESH, WHO CUT OUT THE BULL'S HEART AND GAVE IT AS AN OFFERING TO SHAMASH, THE SUN GOD.

IN GREEK MYTHOLOGY THE MINOTAUR WAS HALF-MAN, HALF-BULL. HE LIVED DEEP IN A MAZE ON THE ISLAND OF CRETE AND EACH YEAR DEVOURED SEVEN YOUTHS AND SEVEN MAIDENS SENT AS A TRIBUTE BY THE ATHENIANS TO THEIR MASTER, KING MINOS OF CRETE. THESEUS, SON OF THE KING OF ATHENS, VOWED TO STOP THE SLAUGHTER. USING A BALL OF WOOL THAT HE UNRAVELLED AS HE WENT INTO THE MAZE AND WHOSE TRAIL HE FOLLOWED ON HIS RETURN, THESEUS SUCCEEDED IN KILLING THE MINOTAUR. KING MINOS ALSO OWNED A BULL WITH THE STAR, ALDEBARAN, ON ITS FOREHEAD. WHEN MINOS RENEGED ON AN AGREEMENT TO SACRIFICE THE BULL TO POSEIDON, POSEIDON DROVE THE BULL MAD SO THAT IT RAMPAGED OVER THE ISLAND OF CRETE, DESTROYING EVERYTHING IN ITS PATH. IN DESPERATION, MINOS CALLED IN HERCULES, THE TROUBLESHOOTER OF THE ANCIENT WORLD, WHO CAPTURED THE BULL, THUS RIDDING MINOS OF HIS TERRIBLE PROBLEM.

THE BULL'S DEATH OR CAPTURE IN THESE STORIES SYMBOLISES THE DEFEAT OF WINTER DARKNESS BY THE FORCES OF LIGHT. IT ALSO REPRESENTS THE DEFEAT OF THE 'BEAST WITHIN' — THE TRIUMPH OF REASON OVER BRUTE STRENGTH, OR A METAPHOR FOR THE PROGRESS WE MAKE FROM BEING HELPLESS BABIES AT THE MERCY OF OUR NEEDS, TO BECOMING WELL-INTEGRATED MEMBERS OF SOCIETY, AWARE OF THE NEEDS OF OTHERS. IT CAN ALSO BE INTERPRETED ON A MORE SPIRITUAL LEVEL: WE MUST LEARN TO OVERCOME AND TRANSCEND EARTHLY DESIRES, REPLACING THEM WITH SPIRITUAL ENLIGHTENMENT.

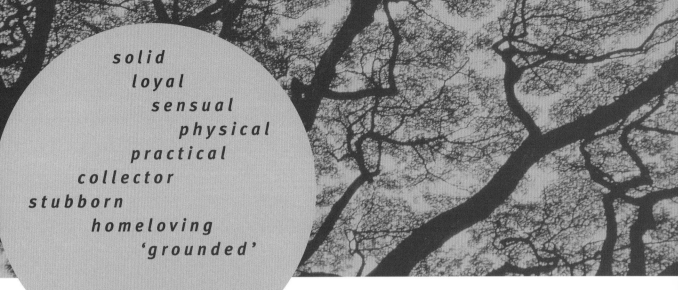

solid
loyal
sensual
physical
practical
collector
stubborn
homeloving
'grounded'

white, blue, green, copper, coral

Taurus's animal, the bull, represents many of the characteristics associated with this sign. It is a huge, lumbering beast that can be solid, steady and even cumbersome one minute, but destructive and wild the next. Yet Taurus is said to be faithful, loyal and steadfast, and many who have benefited from friendship with a Taurean could wish for no better companion. Taurean constancy – it is, after all, a Fixed sign – also means that Taurus tends to hang on to the past. This has its positive side: Taurus is good at preserving the best of the past. The downside, of course, is that Taurus often demonstrates a dogged attachment to negative courses of action, frequently refusing to see others' point of view or to make improvements that are patently necessary.

Taurus is also classified as an Earth sign and is ruled by Venus, the planet of love and affection, hence its sensual, earthy reputation and its associations with fertility. Earth and Venus also confer a love of beauty, an appreciation of the arts and a fondness for indulgence. This last trait may be expressed in very different ways. Taurus can be either glutton or a gourmet; he or she may be preoccupied with the pursuit of private pleasure, or may be eager to give enjoyment to others. In some cases, Taureans' enthusiasm for overindulgence can manifest itself as materialism and, when this happens, they have the unnerving habit of judging people according to appearances or the size of their bank balance. To counteract this tendency, Taurus could take its cue from Scorpio, its opposite sign. Scorpio is singularly unimpressed by materialism: it is much more interested in people who express their thoughts and feelings with passion.

The Earth, like the bull or the cow, brings associations of heaviness, solidity and passivity. But to accuse Taurus of inertia, of always waiting for others to make the first move, is often a misunderstanding. If Taurus appears to

be simply going along with what others want, it may be because it does not feel strongly enough about the alternatives on offer. Or it may just be because it lacks the confidence to express its own desires.

The Earth also confers practical skills. This means that Taureans are frequently adept at seeing what can realistically be achieved in life, but it also brings dexterity in the sense of being good at mending and making things. What Taureans perhaps lack is a little creativity. For this they might look at the two signs that lie half way between Taurus and Scorpio. The first of these, Leo, can give Taurus a lesson in how to be brilliantly creative, while the second, Aquarius, can demonstrate how the mind may be opened to new possibilities.

Some notable people, past and present, who were born with the Sun in Taurus include the last tsar of Russia, Nicholas II, Salvador Dalí, Barbra Streisand, William Shakespeare, Shirley Temple, Al Pacino and Karl Marx.

Taurus's relationships

With Venus as its ruling planet, Taurus is a sociable and friendly sign, while, as a sign of sensual gratification, it can make an exciting partner. However, when Taurus places more emphasis on receiving pleasure than on giving it, relationships are bound to run into difficulties. Sooner or later, partners will feel ignored or taken for granted, so Taureans should make a conscious effort to make them feel loved and cherished.

Taurus's emphasis on materialism and the value it places on appearances can intrude on its relationships. It can, for example, lead Taurus to make superficial judgements about people and it can also make it sometimes treat

venus

RULED BY VENUS, THE PLANET —
AND GODDESS — OF LOVE, TAURUS
IS A SIGN OF SENSUAL GRATIFICATION
AND SELF-INDULGENCE. VENUS WAS
RENOWNED FOR HER NUMEROUS
LOVE AFFAIRS.

the bull

TAURUS IS REPRESENTED BY THE BULL, A POWERFUL BEAST
THAT IS SLOW TO ROUSE BUT ONCE PROVOKED IS FEARSOME.
WORDS AND PHRASES SUCH AS 'BULLY', 'BULL IN A CHINA SHOP'
AND 'LIKE A RED RAG TO A BULL' ARE VIVID IMAGES OF TAURUS
WHEN ANGRY. PARADOXICALLY, TAURUS CAN ALSO BE STUBBORN.
ONCE SOMEONE OR SOMETHING HAS ANNOYED IT, IT CAN
NURSE A GRIEVANCE FOR YEARS. ITS STUBBORNNESS
OFTEN LEADS IT TO REFUSE TO CHANGE ITS WAYS
— EVEN WHEN CHANGE IS WHAT IS
NEEDED.

its partner as just another possession – and one of which it is obsessively jealous. Whatever form the materialism takes, it is a recipe for disaster. Instead, Taurus should make an effort to truly understand the loved one and to respect his or her independence.

No astrologer expects the sparks to fly when two Taureans get together for, after all, when two rock-solid, security-loving individuals form a relationship, the result should be even more stability and security. But things do not always work out that way, for when two obstinate people have ideas that are fundamentally opposed, it may be impossible for them ever to compromise. There is, therefore, no way of predicting whether two Taureans might fall deeply in love or form a lifelong antipathy to one another.

Relationships with Virgo and Capricorn, the other two Earth signs, are said to be easier, partly because they share sufficient similarities to be able to reach agreement where necessary, but also because they enjoy the different perspectives each brings to the relationship. Like Taurus, both Virgo and Capricorn possess conservative qualities and a practical disposition. While Taurus brings a sense of stability to the relationship, Virgo contributes its skill in dealing with detail and Capricorn confers its good business sense.

Taurus's relationships with the Water signs – Scorpio, Cancer and Pisces – can be close and affectionate. Of these, relationships with Scorpio may be the most compulsive because the signs are opposites. The one's

life-enhancing strategies

- REMEMBER THAT TRUE SECURITY COMES FROM BUILDING UP YOUR SELF-CONFIDENCE, NOT FROM RELYING ON MATERIAL COMFORT OR WEALTH.

- YOU CAN BE TOO PASSIVE AND MAY SOMETIMES HAVE ALLOWED SOMEONE TO GET THEIR WAY SIMPLY BECAUSE YOU REMAINED SILENT. AFTERWARDS, YOU HAVE REGRETTED IT, SO NEXT TIME YOU ARE IN A SIMILAR SITUATION, TRY TO ENSURE THAT YOU EXPRESS YOUR OPINION AND THAT WHAT YOU FEEL IS TAKEN INTO ACCOUNT.

- OWN YOUR POSSESSIONS. DO NOT LET THEM OWN YOU.

- MONEY IS IMPORTANT TO YOU, BUT DO NOT GET SUCKED INTO A STRESSED, PRESSURISED, WORK-DOMINATED LIFESTYLE JUST BECAUSE YOU THINK YOU NEED TO EARN THE MONEY. IT WOULD BE FAR HEALTHIER TO FIND A MORE SATISFYING OR CREATIVE LINE OF WORK, EVEN IF IT MEANS EARNING LESS AND CUTTING YOUR EXPENDITURE.

- REMEMBER YOUR STRENGTHS — RELIABILITY AND A REALISTIC SENSE OF WHAT IS ACHIEVABLE — AND CAPITALISE ON THEM TO PROVIDE A FEELING OF SECURITY FOR FAMILY AND FRIENDS.

- IF YOU ARE FRIGHTENED BY CHANGE, THINK ABOUT WHAT IT IS IN THE PROPOSED CHANGE THAT ALARMS YOU. ONCE YOU HAVE WORKED OUT WHAT THE PROBLEM REALLY IS, YOU HAVE TAKEN THE FIRST STEP TOWARDS SOLVING IT. TALK ABOUT IT TO PEOPLE AND SEE IF, BY BRINGING IT OUT INTO THE OPEN, YOU CAN FEEL LESS ANXIOUS.

strengths compensate perfectly for the other's weaknesses, with Scorpio providing the inner dimension and emotional intensity, and Taurus dealing with the outer reality and the demands of everyday life. Both Scorpio and Taurus make long-term commitments, but the balance is a delicate one and if the signs fall out, Taurus may become bored with Scorpio's moods while Scorpio can be disillusioned by what it sees as Taurus's superficiality.

Relationships with Cancer and Pisces are often less compulsive and less passionate, but they are more likely to lead to lasting friendship. Taurus gives both these signs stability and the feeling that it will always be there for them, while they give Taurus a sense of emotional purpose and some meaning to life.

The three Air signs – Gemini, Libra and Aquarius – often regard Taurus with bewilderment. These three signs occupy the realms of ideas and communication, so they

sometimes just do not grasp what Taurus, with its earthy sensuality, is driving at, but these differences can make for a good relationship. Gemini will bring its sense of lively curiosity to a relationship with Taurus. Libra – the Air sign that is most similar to Taurus – will contribute its ability to mould a harmonious environment. Aquarius, meanwhile, will challenge Taurus to face up to new ideas or experiment with a fresh way of life.

Taurus's relationships with the three Fire signs – Aries, Leo and Sagittarius – are not exactly straightforward, but can be surprisingly successful. Aries can find Taurus's cautious ways frustrating, while Taurus becomes exasperated with what it sees as Aries' bossiness, its excessive willingness to take risks and its refusal to consider the facts. Meanwhile, Taurus provides Aries with emotional stability and Aries contributes its adventurous instincts, ambition and enthusiasm. Taurus and Leo are both obstinate signs, so as long as they share a common goal, they get on marvellously, but as soon as their aspirations diverge, they can fall out. Taurus and Sagittarius can be magical together just as long each respects the other's differences – such as the fact that Sagittarius will probably want to wander the world while Taurus will prefer to stay at home. The two will have to find a way of working this one out!

Taurus' s health and wellbeing

Robust health and a strong constitution are frequent features of the Taurean personality. However, traditionally, Taurus has a special association with the throat and neck – people born with this sign strongly in their chart are reputed to be good singers or, at the very least, to enjoy singing – so the typical Taurean complaint is a sore throat. In the ancient medical tradition, soreness was categorised as a 'hot' complaint and was associated with

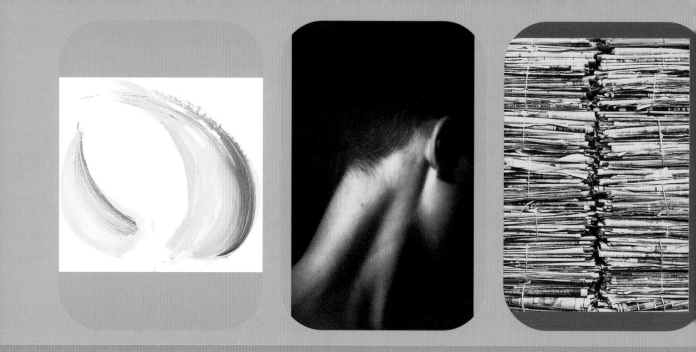

the red-hot planet Mars. Some forms of complementary healing such as homeopathy suggest that the cure for soreness is to use fiery Martian remedies, in the belief that the 'hot' remedy cancels out the 'hot' complaint. The classic remedy for a sore throat, therefore, is to slice an onion very thinly and cover it with honey. The juice from the onion bleeds into the honey, and the resulting liquid is then drunk. It is said to provide instant relief. Ginger and honey tea, preferably made with freshly chopped root ginger, has a similar effect.

With its tendency towards solidity, passivity and placidity, Taurus is not normally associated with vigorous exercise, so sports which require aggression or speed often leave poor Taurus trailing. Instead, gentle exercises such as T'ai Chi or bowls will suit it better. In fact, many Taureans are happier keeping fit without taking up a sport at all. Such people may prefer gardening – a classic Taurean activity. But the sad fact is that Taurus's most famous weakness is its laziness, which means that its favourite activity is often having a doze in a comfortable chair. While this may not do much for the Taurean metabolic rate, Taureans can take comfort from the fact that they are often more relaxed and less prone to stress than the more energetic signs.

Because Taurus is prone to overindulge in food and drink, it needs to take care of its digestive system. A first step can be to try replacing rich foods with salads and lean meat, and to avoid excessive alcohol. Fortunately for them, Taureans often eat slowly and this is a distinct advantage when it comes to ensuring good digestion.

As a lover of comfort and beauty, Taurus is very interested in its environment. It appreciates the soothing qualities of gently harmonious colours – soft browns and greens, perhaps mixed with a little white – and enjoys

being surrounded by calming greenery and white and yellow flowers. It also likes flowers that have a sweet aroma to lift the spirits and add to one's sense of wellbeing. In the home, comfortable furniture is probably its first priority, but being surrounded by beautiful objects is also important, especially if these are of sentimental value. Many Taureans hate to throw away even old and useless things. The result is that some Taurean homes can come to resemble museums of weird and wonderful objects collected from anywhere and everywhere – but amid all that you can be sure that comfort will prevail.

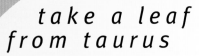

take a leaf from taurus

BEING AN EARTH SIGN, TAURUS IS TRADITIONALLY CONNECTED WITH
FERTILITY. THAT PLUS ITS PRACTICAL NATURE MEAN THAT TAUREANS TAKE
NATURALLY TO GARDENING. DEVELOP THE TAUREAN IN YOU BY DOING SOME
GARDENING. IN THE NORTHERN HEMISPHERE, THIS IS THE IDEAL TIME OF YEAR
FOR PLANTING SEEDS. SEEING THEM GROW INTO FULL-SIZED PLANTS
IS A WONDERFUL WAY OF GETTING IN TOUCH WITH THE
EARTH AND WITH THE RHYTHMS OF NATURE. YOU DO
NOT NEED A GARDEN TO BE A GARDENER. A
SMALL BACK YARD OR EVEN A WINDOW
BOX OR SUNNY WINDOW SILL
WILL DO PERFECTLY.

festivals

Taurus being a pleasure-loving, indulgent sign, it is not
surprising that its time of year – and May in particular (May is known
as the 'merry month') – is a time of much merrymaking. May Day is a day whose traditions of wild pleasure have
lived on into modern times in the celebration of 1 May as a workers' festival. Before the fall of communism, May
Day was celebrated most notably with the great military parades in Moscow's Red Square.

May Day's origins lie in Beltane, the ancient Celtic festival fixed for 30 April or 1 May, approximately midway
between the spring equinox and the summer solstice. Beltane is named after Bel (meaning 'bright' or 'shining'),
a Celtic solar deity, and 'tane' meaning 'fire'. One custom during the celebration of Beltane involved driving
livestock between two fires in a purification rite and as protection against disease. Another theory is that 'tane'
is derived from 'dine' meaning cattle, because newborn calves were sacrificed on this day. Whatever the truth,
May Day celebrations were always riotous affairs in which normal sexual taboos could be broken. This aspect of
May Day provides us with another link with Taurus as a sign of fertility.

The greatest

Taurean religious festival

– it takes place at the full moon in

Taurus – is the celebration of Buddha's birth, enlightenment and death. This festival is known as Vesak, Wesak or Vaisaka and is the most sacred date in the Buddhist calendar. The festival features the setting free of birds, which symbolise humanity's connection to the cosmic order and the flight of ideas to heaven. In Malaysia, white doves are released and celebrants gather at dawn at the temples for religious ceremonies. In Sri Lanka, the date is marked by the lighting of lanterns, to symbolise the light of enlightenment. During the festival, particular stress is laid on Buddha's enlightenment and teaching, which stated that all suffering is the result of desire. Taurus might do well to observe that perhaps some of its problems are caused by greed and frustration.

a meditation

TAURUS NEEDS A SLOW LIFESTYLE AND IS OFTEN OUT OF SYMPATHY WITH THE HIGH-PRESSURE DEMANDS OF MODERN LIFE. THIS MEDITATION IS PERFECT FOR TAUREANS WHO ARE SUFFERING FROM A SURFEIT OF PROFESSIONAL AND FAMILY PRESSURES.

Lie down or sit comfortably and close your eyes. Imagine your everyday life: the alarm clock going off, getting to work, the traffic jams and crowded buses and trains, the constant meetings, phone calls and deadlines. Now imagine you are walking down a city street. Gradually you notice that there are fewer people and cars, less noise and bustle. You turn the corner and the buildings come to an end. All that is left are a few rustic cottages. Ahead lie meadows and woods. There is long grass, wild flowers, hedges and trees. Birds fly overhead. You wander along, breathing in the sweet air, then lie down in the grass and rest. When you are ready, you slowly walk back to the city. Once there, the city's hustle and bustle no longer bothers you. You can cope with the demands on your time because your rural paradise lives on inside you. You can revisit it whenever you want.

constellation

TAURUS, THE BULL OF HEAVEN, IS ONE OF THE MOST VISIBLE CONSTELLATIONS. ITS BRIGHTEST FEATURE IS THE SIX (SOME SAY SEVEN) STARS OF THE PLEIADES, WHICH ARE EASY TO SPOT IN THE EVENING SKY IN AUTUMN AND WINTER. JUST TO THE LEFT OF THE PLEIADES LIES THE GREAT TRIANGLE OF STARS WHICH REPRESENTS THE BULL'S HEAD AND HORNS, OF WHICH THE MOST FAMOUS IS ALDEBARAN, THE ORIGINAL 'BULL'S EYE'.

taurus introduces us to the world of creativity and the pleasures of life

mithraism

ONE OF THE GREATEST OF THE BULL RELIGIONS WAS MITHRAISM, WHICH FLOURISHED IN THE ROMAN EMPIRE. MITHRAS WAS THE CENTRAL CHARACTER IN ONE OF THE GREAT MYSTERY TEACHINGS IN WHICH THE TRIUMPH OF THE SUN IN SPRING WAS REPRESENTED BY MITHRAS, THE SOLAR HERO, SLAYING TAURUS, THE BULL OF HEAVEN. THE DEATH OF THE BULL SIGNIFIED THE LIBERATION OF THE SPIRIT FROM EARTHLY CONSTRAINTS. ADHERENTS TO MITHRAISM HAD TO PASS THROUGH A SERIES OF INITIATIONS. AFTER THE FINAL TEST — THE RITUALS OF SATURN — IT WAS BELIEVED THE SOUL MADE CONTACT WITH THE STARS. THE INITIATED WERE THEN SAID TO HAVE REACHED A STATE OF ENLIGHTENMENT OR OF ONENESS WITH GOD.

gemini

mutable, air, male

GEMINI IS THE SIGN OF THE TWINS, THE SIGN IN WHICH THE SOLAR JOURNEY REACHES THE STAGE AT WHICH LIFE'S DIFFERENT OPTIONS CAN BE IDENTIFIED. IT EXPLORES FRESH POSSIBILITIES AND REVEALS NEW ANSWERS TO OLD PROBLEMS. GEMINI ALSO REPRESENTS DUALITY IN ALL AREAS. IN MORALITY GOOD COMES INTO CONFLICT WITH EVIL, IN RELIGION GODS BATTLE WITH DEMONS, AND IN PSYCHOLOGY, CONSCIOUS CHOICES COMPETE WITH UNCONSCIOUS INSTINCTS. GEMINI'S WEAKNESSES ARE ITS TENDENCY TO BE PULLED BETWEEN IRRECONCILABLE OPTIONS AND ITS INABILITY TO PUT ITS IDEAS INTO ACTION, BUT ITS STRENGTHS ARE ITS SKILL IN RESOLVING CONTRADICTIONS AND ITS FLEXIBILITY.

GEMINI MYTHS CONCERN TWINS OR

SIBLINGS. ONE OF THE EARLIEST IS THE BIBLE STORY OF CAIN

AND ABEL, SONS OF ADAM AND EVE. FOR SOME REASON THAT IS NOT

EXPLAINED, GOD TREASURED ABEL'S SACRIFICES OF SHEEP BUT IGNORED CAIN'S

OFFERINGS OF FRUIT AND VEGETABLES. TORMENTED BY JEALOUSY, CAIN MURDERED HIS

BROTHER. AFTER THIS, GOD CONDEMNED CAIN TO WANDER THE EARTH AS A FUGITIVE.

JEALOUSY WAS ALSO A PROBLEM FOR ROMULUS AND REMUS, THE TWINS OF ROMAN MYTHOLOGY

WHO DECIDED TO FOUND A CITY. WHEN THE GODS INDICATED THAT ROMULUS SHOULD TAKE THE

LEAD, REMUS WAS SCORNFUL, SO ROMULUS KILLED HIM. THE CITY WAS THE CITY OF ROME.

YUREE AND WANJEL WERE AUSTRALIAN ABORIGINAL BROTHERS. WHEN WANJEL WAS KILLED BY A

SNOW. YUREE WAS SO SORROWFUL THAT HE

CARVED HIS BROTHER'S LIKENESS

FROM A TREE TRUNK AND

MADE IT COME TO

LIFE.

JUNGIAN

PSYCHOLOGISTS INTERPRET STORIES OF

THE 'MYTHICAL TWIN' AS A METAPHOR FOR THE

INDIVIDUAL'S SEARCH FOR THEIR 'OTHER' OR THEIR 'SHADOW' —

THOSE ASPECTS OF ONE'S PERSONALITY THAT ONE REFUSES TO

RECOGNISE AND THAT ONE INSTEAD PROJECTS ONTO OTHERS. SO, WHEN

A PERSON FALLS OBSESSIVELY IN LOVE WITH ANOTHER, IT IS SOMETIMES

BECAUSE THEY VALUE IN THE LOVED ONE THE QUALITIES THEY IMAGINE THEY

LACK. PSYCHOLOGISTS BELIEVE THAT IT IS THIS SHADOW SIDE OF PEOPLE THAT

EMERGES AT CRITICAL MOMENTS AND CAUSES THEM TO ACT OUT OF CHARACTER

OR TO ENGAGE IN DESTRUCTIVE ACTS. THEY ARGUE THAT THE FIRST STEP

TOWARDS PSYCHOLOGICAL HEALTH IS FOR PEOPLE TO RECOGNISE THEIR

SHADOW SIDE — A PROCESS KNOWN AS INDIVIDUATION. SOME

FORMS OF PSYCHOTHERAPY ARE GEARED TOWARDS HELPING

PEOPLE GO THROUGH THIS PROCESS.

communicator
changeable
questioning
versatile
nervous
dual nature
inquiring
two-faced
quick-witted

opalescent, mercury, agate

Astrologers describe Gemini as a mutable Air sign. Mutable means changeable and it is said that people born under this sign are infinitely adaptable, constantly able to fit in with changing circumstances. And, as 'air' suggests, Gemini is supposed to be as free as the wind, flitting first one way and then the other. All this talk of adaptability and personal freedom sounds marvellous, but the downside of it is that Gemini people often duck and dive and cancel arrangements at the last minute if it suits them, regardless of the inconvenience to others.

Air does not only signify freedom, though. It can also be seen as a metaphor for the mind and for the lively curiosity and communication skills that Gemini possesses. The typical Gemini individual adores facts, loves finding things out, going places and seeing things, can be a voracious reader, has a brain as sharp as any computer and is happy to talk to anyone. Gemini loves to analyse the world and explain it – to itself and to others. It is a writer, a teacher, a traveller – a sign that will go to any lengths to satisfy its curiosity. Not surprisingly, it can be entertaining company, but it always needs variety and if it has to settle for a life of routine responsibilities, it always needs to have an escape route.

Gemini's symbol – the twins – embodies its dual nature. This makes Gemini well suited to reconciling opposites, resolving contradictions and juggling competing claims on its time and affections. But a weakness is its tendency to spread itself too thin, to be endlessly sidetracked and to promise much but deliver little.

Through its ruling planet, Mercury – the Roman god Mercury was a mischievous, spontaneous character, labelled 'the trickster' by psychologist C. G. Jung – Gemini is also linked to the psychological archetype of the

mercury

THE PLANET MERCURY IS USUALLY SO CLOSE TO THE SUN THAT IT IS OFTEN DIFFICULT TO SPOT. IN FACT, IT IS INVISIBLE TO THE NAKED EYE FOR MUCH OF THE YEAR. PERHAPS THE MYSTERY SURROUNDING ITS PRESENCE IS THE REASON WHY IT HAS LONG BEEN ASSOCIATED WITH MAGICAL MATTERS AND DIVINE COMMUNICATION. IT WAS SAID TO ENCOURAGE WISDOM, TO ASSIST IN THE SEARCH FOR KNOWLEDGE OF THE FUTURE AND TO INSPIRE POETRY. SO WHILE GEMINIANS MIGHT SHINE AS COMMUNICATORS OF OTHERS' IDEAS OR AS TEACHERS, THEY ARE ALSO SUITED TO BEING WRITERS — OR EVEN ASTROLOGERS. IF YOU ARE A GEMINI AND DREAM OF BEING A POET OR OF WRITING A NOVEL, HOW ABOUT SIGNING UP FOR A CREATIVE WRITING COURSE? IT COULD BE THE FIRST STEP!

puer eternus, or 'eternal youth'. In other words, Gemini sometimes, just like Peter Pan, simply refuses to grow up. While the other signs are often attracted to Gemini for its youthful charm and playful manner, Gemini may exploit this by choosing partners who unconsciously play the 'parent', taking charge of the important things in life and leaving Gemini free to indulge its whims.

Famous people who were born with the Sun in Gemini include John F. Kennedy, Queen Victoria, Marilyn Monroe, Dante, Che Guevara, Kylie Minogue, Bob Dylan, Judy Garland, Paul McCartney, Anne Frank, Philip II of Spain and Al Jolson.

Gemini's relationships

Just as duality is a Geminian theme, so in their relationships, Gemini people seem to be constantly searching for their 'mythical twin'. One expression of this 'mythical twin' idea can be found in the Talmud, the Hebrew commentary on the Bible, where it is written that a soul can become divided, one half being given to a boy, the other to a girl. The two halves spend their lives seeking each other out.

And so it is that Geminians appear to be always looking for a soulmate. You will often find them surrounded by large groups of people as though they feel that the more people they meet, the more likely they are to find the one special person to be with. They use their charm and wit to flatter potential lovers and they beguile

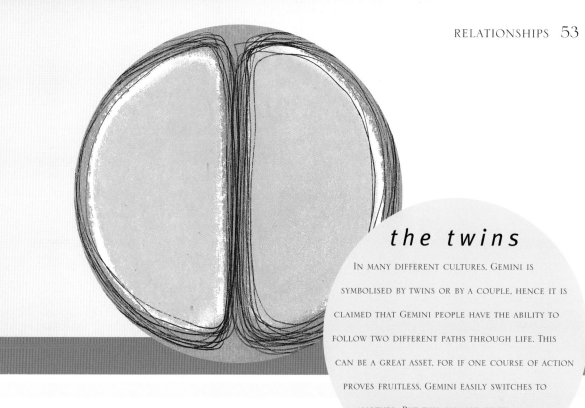

the twins

them with their mercurial minds. They also have a reputation for flirting and falling in and out of love with an ease that leaves the other signs gasping. But this is all grist to Gemini's mill for, paradoxically, it is sometimes said that the typical Gemini will seek out different people to satisfy different needs.

Ultimately, though, Gemini is a sign that thrives best in a one-to-one relationship – the right individual seems to make Gemini feel whole, as if it has found the part of itself that it was searching for. At the end of the day, perhaps what Gemini was looking for lay within itself all along, but maybe Gemini, like all of us, has a tendency to begin by looking for the answers in other people.

With their analytical minds, Gemini people often have strong ideas as to how relationships should be conducted. They consider any problems that may arise and work out what must be done in everyone's interest. Many of them also devote a great deal of energy to analysing their and others' feelings rather than to simply experiencing them, then they are sometimes taken aback to discover that they and their lovers are messy flesh-and-blood creatures with real-life passions. Gemini's challenge in life is to explore the world of emotions and harness the power of human passion.

This aspect of Gemini helps to explain its relationships with the other signs, and especially with the three Water signs – Cancer, Scorpio and Pisces. In these relationships, Gemini can be fascinated, though sometimes embarrassed, by Water's public displays of emotion, while Water, for its part, is intrigued by Gemini's

- YOU THRIVE ON VARIETY BUT YOUR TENDENCY TO CHOP AND CHANGE WITHOUT WARNING IS UNSETTLING FOR OTHERS. MAKE SURE THAT YOU LET PEOPLE KNOW IF YOU CHANGE YOUR PLANS.

- NOURISH YOUR GEMINIAN INSTINCTS, EVEN IN THE FACE OF LIFE'S PRESSURES. TAKE TIME OUT FOR READING, THINKING, GOING FOR A WALK, TALKIN INGS JUST FOR THE PLEASURE OF IT.

- SOMETIMES YOU PROMISE TOO MUCH TO TOO MANY AND END UP LETTING SOME OR ALL OF THEM DOWN. TRY AND CURB YOUR NATURAL INSTINCT TO BE ALL THINGS TO ALL PEOPLE AND ONLY OFFER TO DO WHAT YOU KNOW YOU CAN COMFORTABLY ACHIEVE.

- TRY TO REALLY FEEL WHAT LIES BEHIND PEOPLE'S FEELINGS — AND YOUR OWN — INSTEAD OF OVER-ANALYSING THEM AND SO EXPLAINING THEM AWAY.

- NEVER DOUBLE-BOOK YOURSELF AND ALWAYS BE PUNCTUAL.

- DO YOU EASILY SLIP INTO PLAYING THE CHILD, ALLOWING YOURSELF TO BE IRRESPONSIBLE WHILE YOUR PARTNER DOES ALL THE WORK? IF SO, TAKE RESPONSIBILITY FOR SPECIFIC TASKS — AND GIVE YOUR LOVED ONE A BREAK.

- RATHER THAN RESENTING YOUR PARTNER FOR HOLDING YOU BACK, EXPLAIN HOW YOU SOMETIMES NEED TO FEEL FREE AND HAVE SPACE TO DO YOUR OWN THING. THAT DOES NOT MEAN THAT YOU DO NOT WANT TO BE WITH HIM OR HER, JUST THAT YOU NEED OCCASIONALLY SOME TIME TO YOURSELF.

apparently clear head and rational spirit. Gemini's bright ideas often encourage Cancer to pursue its ambitions, while Gemini is intrigued by Cancer's emotional depths. Similarly, Gemini can be fascinated, though sometimes intimidated, by Scorpio's intensity, while Scorpio admires Gemini's ability to detach itself from its emotions. Gemini and Pisces together make a mutual admiration society for Gemini's clear head is the perfect complement to Pisces' dreamy, spiritual imagination.

Traditionally, Gemini is compatible with Libra and Aquarius, its fellow Air signs, but the truth is not always so simple. While they often share a common outlook on the world, sometimes the spark necessary for a more vibrant relationship is absent. Gemini appreciates Libra's social graces, though not its indecision. If they live together, Gemini will be happy to let Libra get on with the task of creating a pleasant home. Relationships between Gemini and Aquarius make for a wild, creative, adventurous lifestyle, for each encourages the other's freedom-loving instincts.

When two Geminis get together the results can be unpredictable. They may fall madly in love, having sensed that they have each found a soulmate, but they can just as easily feel deeply ill at ease in the relationship, seeing the other person as a mirror-image of themselves, reflecting back their own insecurities and weaknesses. And since Gemini likes its partner to play the parent, another Gemini may not fit the bill.

The three Fire signs – Aries, Leo and Sagittarius – all possessed of glittering energy and enthusiasm, can supply the spark that is sometimes absent between Gemini and the Air signs. Yet relationships with Fire can be explosive. Partnerships between Gemini and Aries are based on a common need for constant experimentation – moving home, changing careers, swapping roles. Gemini and Leo may get on as long as Gemini's enthusiasm for change coincides with Leo's desire to have everything its own way. Gemini-Sagittarius relationships, meanwhile, can be sheer magic as each encourages the other's adventurous nature and reluctance to be tied down. But if that is all holding them together, the relationship can flare up – then fizzle out.

Relationships with the Earth signs – Taurus, Virgo and Capricorn – usually bring more stability, although Gemini may find it hard to conform to Earth's solid, workaday approach to life. Gemini-Taurus partnerships are based on the attraction of opposites, with Gemini providing the spark and Taurus the ability to handle the routine responsibilities of everyday life. Gemini and Virgo can enjoy a very close rapport, for both have bright ideas – and Virgo knows how to put them into practice. Gemini and Capricorn may find each other completely mystifying, for Gemini is full of brilliant ideas while Capricorn values practical experience. But if they do manage to establish a middle ground, theirs can be a relationship that lasts a lifetime.

But it takes two to tango and Gemini is only part of the equation. Others involved – whether at home, at work or in love – need to know how to handle this mercurial sign. The first quality you will need is patience: there is no point complaining about Gemini always being late or taking off at a moment's notice. And if you have children born with the Sun in Gemini, you may suddenly find they have gone off-course. If so, find out why. Maybe some

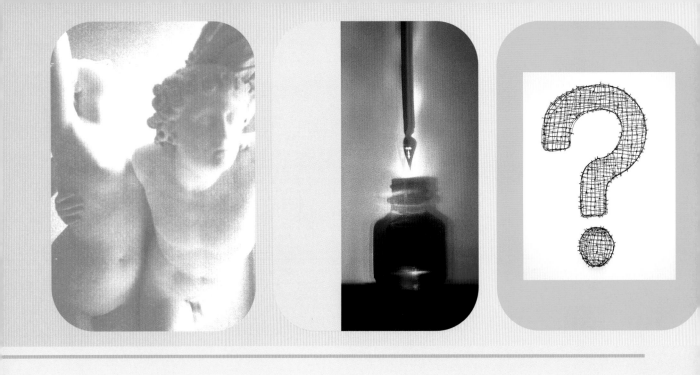

sudden enthusiasm has prompted them to do the totally unexpected. And if you have friends born under Gemini, remember that it always pays to have an alternative plan ready in case they do not turn up as planned. Learn to enjoy their company today, for they may be gone tomorrow.

Gemini's health and wellbeing

In medical astrology Gemini rules the lungs. This fact, plus Gemini's classification as an Air sign, means that possible areas of health concern to Gemini are breathing difficulties such as asthma and bronchitis, as well as 'wind' or indigestion. Singing will help with any breathing problems as it is an extremely effective way of opening the lungs. Gemini might find it useful to learn the methods of breath control practised by classical singers. When it comes to avoiding indigestion, Gemini people could do with making time in their lives for food. Usually they are so busy talking, reading or watching television, they scarcely notice what they're eating.

When it comes to taking some exercise, Gemini is traditionally connected with walking, jogging and running – forms of exercise which satisfy the sign's wanderlust and where correct breathing play an important part.

Gemini is not a sign that is troubled by its surroundings. It is perfectly happy in a busy town or city environment, living on a main road or walking along crowded streets. Often its home can be untidy – a reflection perhaps of its playfulness and its thirst for knowledge. There may be books everywhere or masses of interesting objects that it has picked up on its travels. If you live with someone born with the Sun in Gemini, you may either have to learn to tolerate a higher-than-average level of chaos, or you must get on and do the clearing up.

star of hermes

THE BABYLONIANS BELIEVED THAT GEMINI'S RULING PLANET MERCURY WAS SACRED TO NABU, THE SCRIBE, WHO WROTE DOWN THE DECISIONS OF THE GODS AND GODDESSES. THE GREEKS CALLED MERCURY THE STAR OF HERMES, THE MESSENGER OF THE GODS, AND TWO THOUSAND YEARS AGO GREEK AND EGYPTIAN MYSTICS COMPOSED THE HERMETIC TEACHINGS, ALLEGEDLY WRITTEN BY HERMES HIMSELF. THESE TEXTS WERE REDISCOVERED IN RENAISSANCE EUROPE, WHEN HERMES WAS CONSIDERED TO BE A GREAT TEACHER. THEY PROPOUNDED DOCTRINES SUCH AS THAT OF REINCARNATION, IN WHICH THE REINCARNATED SOUL DESCENDS TO EARTH THROUGH THE STARS AND PLANETS. TO BELIEVERS IT FOLLOWED THAT A PERSON'S SPIRITUAL PURPOSE COULD BE UNDERSTOOD THROUGH CLOSE EXAMINATION OF THEIR HOROSCOPE. THE RESULT WAS A SURGE IN BELIEF IN ASTROLOGY.

festivals

Two of the greatest religious festivals held while the Sun is in Gemini are concerned with communication.

Jews celebrate the festival of Shavuot (meaning 'weeks'). Originally a celebration of the harvesting of the first wheat seven weeks after the harvesting of the first barley, it now commemorates the Revelation of the Law, the moment when Moses was presented with the Ten Commandments on Mount Sinai. Devout Jews stay up all night before Shavuot, studying together and trying to relive the original experience of receiving the Law. On the following day in synagogue, there are readings from Exodus and the 'Akdamut', a special prayer of thanksgiving, is recited.

Pentecost is also concerned with communication. The Acts of the Apostles describes the first Christian Pentecost, relating how Christ's disciples were gathered together in Jerusalem: 'Suddenly a sound came from heaven like the rush of a mighty wind, and it filled all the house...there appeared to them tongues of fire, distributed and resting on each one of them...they were filled with the Holy Spirit and began to speak in tongues as the Spirit gave them utterance'. At the time, Jerusalem was filled with Jews from all over the Mediterranean and Middle East, but each heard the disciples speaking in his or her own language. Peter stood up and proclaimed Jesus to be the Messiah, so Pentecost now commemorates the foundation of the Christian church. To Christians, salvation through Christ is as important, if not more important, than observation of the Law of Moses, and it was on this crucial point that Christianity began to split, Gemini-style, from Judaism.

take a leaf from gemini

DO YOU HAVE A WORRY? (WHO DOESN'T?) TAKE A LEAD FROM GEMINI, AN AIR SIGN. BLOW UP A BALLOON AND TIE IT WITH A LENGTH OF STRING. WRITE YOUR WORRY DOWN ON A PIECE OF PAPER, ATTACH IT TO THE STRING AND LET THE BALLOON FLY OFF, TAKING YOUR WORRY AWAY WITH IT.

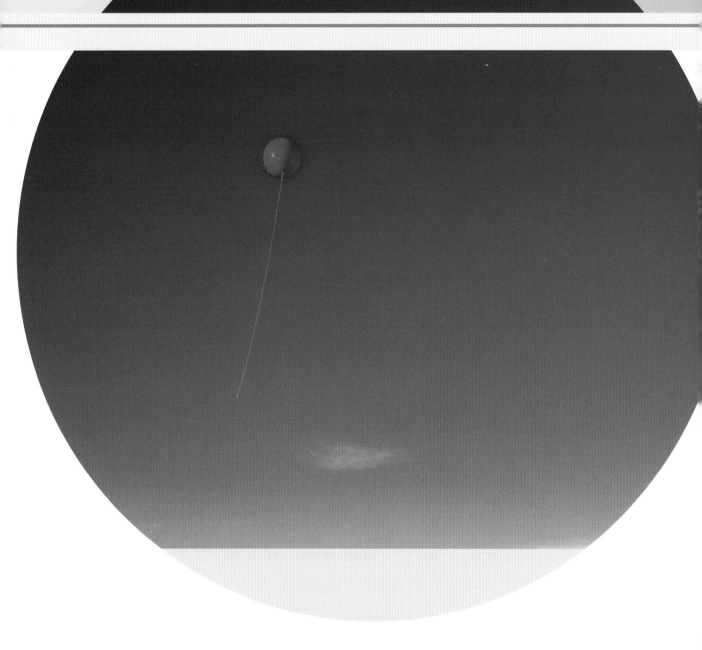

versatile, changeable and lively, Gemini leads us into the realms of

a meditation

GEMINI OFTEN LIVES TOO MUCH IN ITS HEAD AND BUILDS UP AN EXCESS OF NERVOUS ENERGY.
THIS MEDITATION IS DESIGNED TO RESTORE A SENSE OF CALM.

Lie down outside in an open breezy place or, if indoors, near to an open window. Close your eyes and try to make your breathing regular. Gradually become aware of your arms and legs, hands, feet, toes and fingers and the electric flow of nervous energy around them. You may feel your skin tingle. Now observe how your whole nervous system links together smoothly over your body and connects with your mind. You should not feel any blockages. As you lie there, you will become aware of the air around you, clean and fresh, caressing your body, cleansing and rejuvenating it. Try to feel as if you are floating, supported by the wind. Your body's nervous energy extends outwards, to the air around you. Feel this process taking place and notice how it makes you feel happier. When you are ready, begin to come back to earth. When you open your eyes you will feel much calmer, more relaxed and ready to face the world once again.

constellation

GEMINI IS ONE OF THE LARGEST CONSTELLATIONS AND ONE OF THE EASIEST TO SPOT. IN THE LATE EVENING IN JANUARY OR FEBRUARY, LOOK SOUTHWARDS (OR NORTHWARDS IF YOU LIVE IN THE SOUTHERN HEMISPHERE) AND YOU WILL SEE TWO BRIGHT STARS, ONE ABOVE THE OTHER. THEY ARE CASTOR AND POLLUX — NAMED AFTER THE GREEK HERO-TWINS — AND THEY MARK THE HEADS OF THE TWINS OF THE CONSTELLATION. A LITTLE WAY TO THE RIGHT ARE TWO DIMMER STARS, ALSO ONE ABOVE THE OTHER. TOGETHER WITH CASTOR AND POLLUX, THESE FORM A RECTANGLE. TO ANCIENT PEOPLE, THESE TWO PAIRS OF STARS REPRESENTED THE CONTRASTING CHOICES THAT ARE SUCH A FEATURE OF THE SUN SIGN OF GEMINI.

intellectual enquiry, curiosity and communication

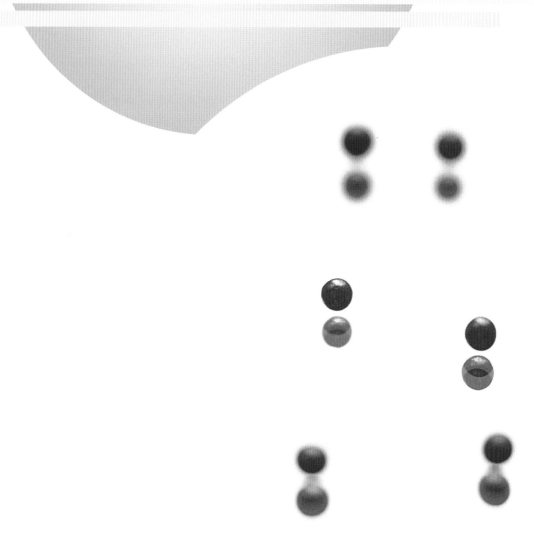

cancer

cardinal, water, female

21 june – 23 july

THE SUN ENTERS CANCER ON 21 JUNE, THE DAY WHEN IT REACHES ITS FURTHEST DISTANCE FROM THE EQUATOR, GIVING THE SHORTEST DAY IN THE SOUTHERN HEMISPHERE AND THE LONGEST DAY IN THE NORTH. THIS DAY OF EXTREMES HINTS AT CANCER'S CONTRADICTORY NATURE — IT IS SHY AND SENSITIVE, YET CONFIDENT AND AMBITIOUS. THE SIGN OF EXCESSIVE EMOTION, CANCER IS OFTEN TOTALLY DOMINATED BY ITS FEELINGS. ITS TASK IS TO LEARN TO THINK CLEARLY. THIS IS NEVER EASY, BUT NO CHALLENGE IS TOO GREAT FOR THE TRUE CANCERIAN. WHEN IT IS EMOTIONALLY COMMITTED TO ITS GOALS, CANCER GIVES ITS ALL TO ACHIEVING SUCCESS.

CANCER'S

MYTHS ARE MOON STORIES. POLYNESIANS TELL

OF HINA, WHOSE NAME MEANS 'MOON'. WHILE BATHING, AN EEL

PASSED BY AND TOUCHED HER. IT TURNED OUT TO BE TE TUNA — A MAN IN

DISGUISE. THEY BECAME LOVERS, BUT ONE DAY TE TUNA TOLD HINA THAT NEXT TIME

HE CAME, SHE SHOULD CUT OFF HIS HEAD AND BURY IT. STRICKEN WITH GRIEF, SHE DID

SO, BUT RETURNED TO THE SPOT EVERY DAY TO MOURN. ONE DAY A GREEN SHOOT APPEARED AT

TE TUNA'S GRAVE. IT EVENTUALLY GREW INTO THE FIRST COCONUT TREE.

THE ANCIENT GREEK MOON GODDESSES WERE SELENE AND ARTEMIS. ARTEMIS WAS ADVENTUROUS AND

SPENT HER DAYS HUNTING. SHE AND THE MAIDENS WHO SERVED HER HAD TAKEN A VOW OF CHASTITY.

ONE DAY, THE PASSIONATE HUNTSMAN, ACTAEON, CAME ACROSS ARTEMIS WHILE SHE WAS BATHING AND

WAS ENTRANCED BY HER BEAUTY. ENRAGED, SHE TURNED HIM INTO A STAG AND HAD HER HOUNDS TEAR

HIM TO PIECES. SELENE WAS MORE AMOROUS. HER FAMOUS LOVER WAS ENDYMION, BY WHOM SHE HAD

FIFTY DAUGHTERS. ENDYMION BEGGED ZEUS FOR IMMORTALITY. THIS WAS GRANTED ON

CONDITION THAT ENDYMION SLEEP FOR EVER, SO EVERY NIGHT

SELENE BATHES HIM IN KISSES, JUST AS THE MOON

BATHES SLEEPING MORTALS

IN ITS COOL,

SOOTHING

LIGHT.

THE

POLYNESIAN MYTH DEALS WITH

THE THEME OF THE EBB AND FLOW OF LIFE

— TE TUNE'S DEATH MEANT A NEW BEGINNING —

AND OF THE NEED TO LET GO OF THE PAST AND MOVE

ON, SOMETHING CANCER OFTEN FINDS EXTREMELY

DIFFICULT TO ACHIEVE. BETWEEN THEM, ARTEMIS AND

SELENE REPRESENT TWO CONTRADICTORY SIDES OF THE

CANCERIAN PERSONALITY — THE ONE BOLD, OUTGOING,

TOUGH AND APPARENTLY SELF-SUFFICIENT; THE

OTHER SOFT, CARING, THOUGHTFUL

AND ALWAYS LOVING.

sensitive
arrogant
tenacious
emotional
compassionate
perfectionist
vulnerable
cleansing
masked

silver, white, crystal

Cancer is an enigma and Cancerians are quite capable of pursuing courses of action which are completely at variance with one another. This makes it one of the most difficult of the zodiac signs to understand, but the key lies in the different categories into which astrologers fit it. It has the distinction of being both a Cardinal sign – capable of taking the lead, controlling its environment and giving the orders – and a Water sign – implying excessive emotion and vulnerability. Astrologers have also designated the crab as Cancer's symbol, a metaphor for the soft centre and hard outer shell of the Cancer personality.

It comes as no surprise then, that while astrology books often talk about romantic, idealistic Cancer, many Cancerian people put on a complaining, cynical, 'crabby' exterior. So if you meet Cancerians who appear to be wrapped up in themselves, you should not condemn them for it. They are almost certainly putting on a front – retreating into their shell – to protect themselves from their anxiety that there is no limit to the amount of compassion that the world requires of them, but that there is a limit to the amount that they are able to supply.

And like a crab, Cancer is tenacious. Once it wants to do something, it will see to it that it achieves its goals whatever the odds. But this tenacity sometimes manifests itself in clinging to the past; it fears what will happen if it lets go. Cancer needs to recognise that there are times in life when it must have the courage to say farewell to former circumstances, and take a leap into the unknown.

Along with its tenacity, Cancer also has a perfectionist streak, a desire always to achieve the very best. The downside of this is that Cancer always worries in case it does not meet its own high standards. In fact, it is

the moon

CANCER'S RULING PLANET, THE MOON, WAS DEFINED BY CLASSICAL ASTRONOMERS AS FEMININE AND BY TRADITIONAL ASTROLOGERS AS THE COSMIC MOTHER. THAT IS WHY THE CANCER PERSONALITY IS USUALLY REGARDED AS CARING AND NURTURING — TIME-HONOURED QUALITIES SAID TO BE POSSESSED BY MOTHERS THE WORLD OVER. BUT TODAY'S CANCER MEN CAN TAKE HEART FROM THE FACT THAT SUCH QUALITIES ARE NOW THOUGHT TO BE JUST AS ESSENTIAL FOR THEM TOO.

earthquakes and lunatics

APART FROM THE SUN, THE MOON INFLUENCES US MORE THAN ANY OTHER CELESTIAL BODY. MOST PEOPLE ARE AWARE THAT THE MOON EXERTS A PULL THAT AFFECTS THE MOVEMENT OF THE TIDES, BUT MANY DO NOT REALISE THAT THE WORLD'S LAND MASSES ARE ALSO SUBJECT TO THE MOON'S PULL, AND THAT THIS IS THOUGHT TO PLAY A PART IN CAUSING EARTHQUAKES. THE DEVASTATING EARTHQUAKE IN TURKEY ON 11 AUGUST 1999 TOOK PLACE JUST A FEW DAYS AFTER THE SOLAR ECLIPSE, WHEN THE MOON PASSED IN FRONT OF THE SUN. IN FACT, THE ECLIPSE HAD PASSED DIRECTLY OVER THE MAIN FAULT LINE IN NORTHERN TURKEY. LESS EASY TO MEASURE IS THE MOON'S EFFECT ON INDIVIDUALS. IT HAS LONG BEEN BELIEVED THAT THE WAXING AND WANING OF THE MOON CAN CAUSE ERRATIC BEHAVIOUR IN PEOPLE — HENCE THE WORD 'LUNATIC' — AND THERE IS NO END OF ANECDOTAL EVIDENCE TO SHOW THAT ACCIDENTS AND IRRATIONAL BEHAVIOUR INCREASE AROUND THE FULL MOON, A FACT TO WHICH HOSPITAL STAFF AND THE POLICE CAN ATTEST.

sometimes said that Cancer people are not happy unless they have something to worry about.

With Cancer being such an enigmatic sign, it is no surprise that the roll call of people born with the Sun in Cancer includes many diverse personalities, among them Sylvester Stallone, Ringo Starr, Princess Diana, Emmeline Pankhurst, Richard Branson, Yul Brynner, Imelda Marcos, John Glenn, Iris Murdoch, Linda Ronstadt, Ernest Hemingway, Meryl Streep and Helen Keller.

Cancer's relationships

The contradictory streak in Cancer shows itself in its relationships. Sometimes it gives the impression it doesn't need other people at all, while at other times it is intensely sociable and even loving. This is because it is often wary of revealing its inner self – it needs to feel it can trust people before it can relax, so it may retreat into its shell and can perhaps appear unfriendly or even hostile. But once Cancer knows it can rely on you, it will be a loyal friend and, in the right circumstances, Cancerian hospitality is legendary and its generosity infinite.

the crab

CANCER'S SYMBOL IS A CRAB, A CREATURE THAT WALKS SIDEWAYS AND SO AVOIDS FACING DIFFICULT PROBLEMS HEAD-ON, BUT IT CAN OFTEN FIND UNUSUAL WAYS ROUND PERSISTENT OBSTACLES. THE CRAB ALSO RETREATS INTO ITS SHELL WHEN THREATENED — JUST AS CANCERIANS DO.

In its intimate relationships, Cancer needs true love, the sort of devotion that transcends time and space. It also requires security, and not just a firm emotional anchor but a stable home and a roof over its head. Often talked of as being 'homemakers' – not a description which appeals to all Cancerians, perhaps because they identify it with old-fashioned ideas of a woman's role – both male and female Cancerians frequently have the knack of creating a welcoming, secure domestic environment. In fact, the idea of 'family' and belonging is extremely important to Cancer and, if its relatives happen to live far away, Cancer will often try to create 'families' of its friends.

The easiest Cancer relationships are frequently with the other two Water signs – Scorpio and Pisces. Both signs are happy to sacrifice themselves for love: the problem can be that they get so caught up in their feelings that they lose touch with real life. And when two Cancerians get together, this flight from reality may be even more complete. Cancer gets along well with Scorpio. If the two drift apart it can be because of a simple failure to talk to each other and because each can be too ready to take offence at imagined slights. Cancer and Pisces can get involved in a similar dynamic and for them, too, it is easy for misunderstandings to pile up. The relationship is saved, though, when each partner genuinely cares for the other and is happy to forgive the other's failings.

Cancer's relationships with its opposite sign, Capricorn, are often close because each provides something the other lacks. Cancer gives love and emotional depth, while Capricorn provides material and financial security. That, at least, is the theory. But if the relationship comes unstuck, Capricorn grows increasingly irritated by what it sees as Cancer's secretive ways and sulky moods, while Cancer is alienated by what it claims is Capricorn's failure to show any real feelings. When it comes to Cancer's relationships with the other Earth signs, those with

life-enhancing strategies

- Do you worry too much? Does your worrying prevent you from doing some of the things you want to do? If so, try to pluck up the courage to talk to someone who can help, for example your family doctor.

- Is there a job you have been putting off for fear of failure? If so, try to make a start on it. Once you get going, your confidence should grow.

- Do you work too hard? Are you finding yourself worn out from too much work and resentful that other people do not offer you help? Learn to separate essential tasks from non-essential ones, the urgent from the non-urgent. Then you must learn to delegate.

- Are you attracted to someone yet worried to make the first move for fear of rejection? If so, remember that being rejected is not the worst thing that can happen in life. If someone turns you down, they are the loser, so have confidence in yourself and take the plunge.

- If you find yourself being harsh or hurtful to others, stop and think why you are doing it. Could it be that you are taking out on them hurts inflicted on you in the past? To improve your relationships, try to find something good to say to or do for other people instead.

- Do not be embarrassed about being a sensitive, emotional, intuitive, compassionate and caring individual. You should be proud of possessing these qualities, but make sure that they do not make you over-solitary and withdrawn.

- Complaining about how terrible life is can sometimes give you an excuse for not taking risks. If you catch yourself doing this, try to stop. Instead, go out, make the most of life and do something you have always wanted to do but have never dared.

Taurus are often based on a shared appreciation of domestic stability and family ties, but the spark of passion can be lacking. Cancer and Virgo are drawn together by their innate caution and their need for security and these two can form a solid relationship, but sometimes, as with Cancer and Taurus, something is missing.

When Cancer gets together with the Fire signs – Aries, Leo and Sagittarius – the results can be exciting, if a little steamy. An Aries-Cancer combination may be based on an instant and intense attraction. However, without the discipline of the Earth signs, the relationship may not last very long. Cancer and Leo often make a theatrical combination, with each sign encouraging the other to express its desires and passions, but they are often not ideally suited to domestic routine. Cancer and Sagittarius can make good friends, but sometimes Cancer's need for security and Sagittarius's love of freedom mean that the two have very different aspirations. A long-term relationship, therefore, must be based on a willingness to let the other go his or her own way for a while.

The three Air signs – Gemini, Libra and Aquarius – not surprisingly provide a different sort of relationship. Cancer can be fascinated by Gemini's ideas, its whimsy and the fresh approach it brings to old problems, while Cancer's emotional intensity is often a turn-on for Gemini. Cancer and Libra are both Cardinal signs and like to be in charge, which means that they need to share the same goals if they are to get on in the long-term. When they do, they often play an equal role in creating a harmonious and pleasant home. Relationships between Cancer and Aquarius are essentially based on differences rather than similarities – Cancer needs security while Aquarius values its independence – and as long as each partner respects the other's right to have his or her own interests, opinions and desires, the course can be set for a lifelong friendship.

As a sign of contradictions, Cancer balances confidence and timidity in equal measure, which makes its reactions difficult to predict. If it is rejected in love, it can respond either with defiance or by turning in on itself and retreating behind its cool, sometimes sophisticated mask. And when things go wrong, it can be dismissive of the other person's concerns and suspicious of their motives. The Cancer who behaves like this is not happy. Look below the surface and you will see that Cancer is really crying out for its partner's love and affection.

Cancer's health and wellbeing

In medical astrology Cancer rules the stomach (one part of the body that seems to suffer excessively if there is any stress or worry in life) and the breasts (a symbol of Cancer's maternal qualities). Many Cancer remedies are, therefore, designed to settle stomach problems and help relieve stress.

They include, for example, arrowroot, which calms the stomach. The root of this plant is a starch that can be bought as a powder and used to thicken sauces or puddings. Lemon balm is a classic Cancer herb. Its leaves can be used to make a tea that soothes the stomach and calms the nerves. Traditionally, it is also said to help with period problems and infertility – providing a further link with family-oriented Cancer. Bilberry, which can be taken as a tea, helps with digestive and nervous complaints, while chamomile tea is another highly effective remedy, very soothing to the stomach and good for sleeplessness – many people regard it as the perfect after-dinner drink. Another Cancerian remedy is onion. In Iran and some parts of India, no meal is complete without a side portion of chopped raw onion as an aid to the digestion. This suggestion could have been plucked straight out of the Cancer cook book.

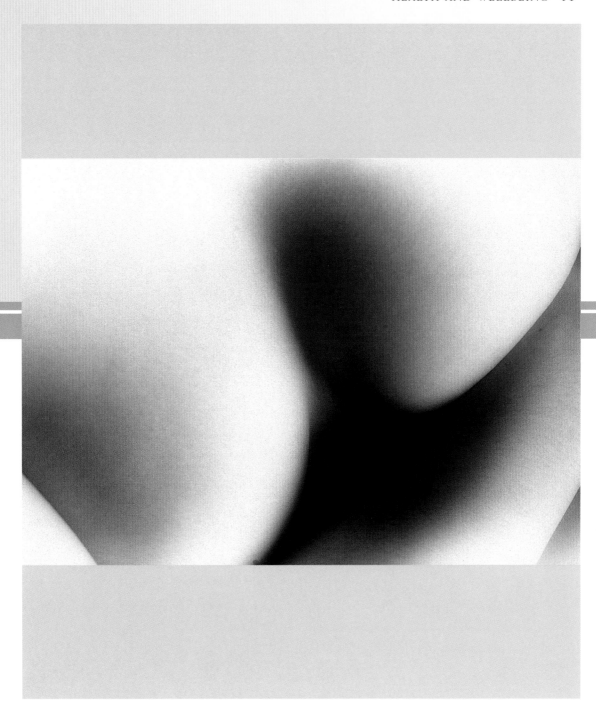

Because Cancerians tend to be such great worriers, they need to do all they can to stay calm. For clothing and the decoration of their homes, they cannot choose better colours than blues and silvers, which are peaceful and easy on the eye. Water – Cancer is, after all, a Water sign – can also be very helpful for calming shattered Cancerian nerves. Swimming is a great form of exercise for them and Cancer people also benefit from visits to natural hot springs and spas. Holidays by the sea bring peace and quiet, but failing that, just having a pond or fountain nearby can work wonders. Putting one in the garden should be high on their list of priorities.

take a leaf from cancer

CANCER PEOPLE LIKE NOTHING MORE THAN MAKING AN EFFORT FOR OTHERS AND THIS IS SOMETHING WE CAN ALL TRY TO DO EVERY DAY. BUT TAKE A LEAF OUT OF CANCER'S BOOK AND DO IT IN STYLE. MAKE THIS A TIME OF YEAR WHEN YOU INVITE FRIENDS AND FAMILY TO A WONDERFUL PARTY. YOUR AIM IS FOR THEM TO FEEL PAMPERED, RELAXED AND AS AT HOME AS POSSIBLE. BUY THE BEST FOOD AND DRINK YOU CAN AFFORD. DON'T FORGET THE FLOWERS. PUT ON SOME MUSIC. INDULGE IN LAVISH TABLE DECORATIONS. PARTY IN THE GARDEN IF YOU CAN. MAKE THIS THE PARTY OF THE YEAR THAT EVERYONE REMEMBERS.

festivals

The Rathra Jatra – or 'chariot journey' – is a summer festival from Orissa in eastern India that is celebrated on the New Moon in Cancer, usually during the rainy season. The festival is sacred to the god Krishna, a manifestation of Siva whose female counterpart is Parvati, the goddess of the Moon and the ruler of Cancer. Krishna is also known by the name of Jagganath – meaning 'Lord of the Universe'. During the celebrations Krishna's devotees push huge wagons (*rathras*) through the streets, topped with flower- and jewel-bedecked images of Krishna and of his brother Balaran, and his sister, Subhadra. The main wagon in the procession is fifteen metres high. Its huge size gives us the English word 'juggernaut' – from Krishna's other name, Jagganath. This enormous wagon also serves to remind us of the fact that Cancer is a tough Cardinal sign – once it gets going, absolutely nothing is allowed to stand in its way!

cancer confers deep and vulnerable emotions, compassion for others

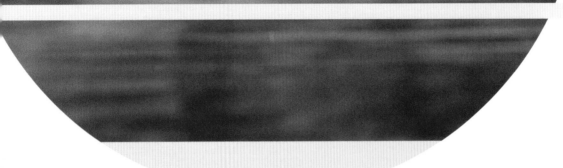

a meditation

THIS MEDITATION WILL APPEAL TO CANCER'S WATERY AND LUNAR ASSOCIATIONS. IT IS ALL ABOUT

ADJUSTING TO THE IDEA THAT SOMETIMES WE HAVE TO GO WITH THE FLOW AND LET GO OF THE

PAST. CANCER MAY BE SURPRISED TO LEARN THAT DOING THIS CAN BRING GREATER SECURITY.

Find a quiet place to lie down and close your eyes. Imagine you are sitting by a lake. The water is calm with just

the occasional ripple caused by a gentle, soothing breeze. You are surrounded by lilies and willows. The Moon

is full and its light glints on the still water. You are part of your entire surroundings. Slowly you feel the water

of the lake lapping around you. It is warm and comfortable. You drift off into the current. As you float, you

gradually feel your cares and worries dissolve. You feel nurtured and restored by the moonlight and the water.

You have a sense of being totally protected. As your worries disappear, your confidence returns. When you

eventually open your eyes, you are ready to face the world again.

constellation

THE CONSTELLATION OF CANCER IS A SMALL ONE
AND NOT EASY TO SPOT. IN FACT, IT LOOKS MORE LIKE AN
INVERTED 'Y' THAN A CRAB! ITS THREE MAIN STARS ARE QUITE
FAINT AND ARE FOUND HALFWAY BETWEEN GEMINI AND LEO.
YOU WILL PROBABLY NEED A STAR MAP TO FIND IT AND A
GOOD CLEAR NIGHT, WELL AWAY FROM CITY LIGHTS. WE
SHOULD REMEMBER THAT THE CANCERIAN CRAB
IS ALSO WELL HIDDEN.

and a love of home and family

leo

fixed, fire, male

24 july – 23 august

THE PROCESS OF CREATION REACHES A CLIMAX IN LEO, FOR THIS IS THE SIGN OF THE SUN, THE SOURCE OF ALL LIFE ON EARTH AND THE CENTRE OF OUR SOLAR SYSTEM. LEO REPRESENTS HIGH NOON, THE PEAK OF ENERGY, THE MOMENT WHEN FERTILITY IS AT ITS PINNACLE AND NATURE IS AT ITS MOST SPLENDID. LIKE THE SUN, LEO IS OFTEN AT THE CENTRE OF THINGS, BUT IT MUST REMEMBER THAT IT IS NOT THE CENTRE OF THE UNIVERSE. THERE ARE TIMES WHEN IT SHOULD STAND ASIDE AND GIVE OTHER PEOPLE A CHANCE. AND JUST AS THE SUN WILL EVENTUALLY BURN ITSELF UP, SO LEO MUST RECOGNISE THAT ITS POWER IS NOT ETERNAL.

THE GREEKS AND ROMANS LINKED THE CONSTELLATION OF LEO TO THE STORY OF HERCULES AND THE NEMEAN LION. IN ANCIENT TIMES, A LION WAS TERRORISING THE PEOPLE OF THE TOWN OF NEMEA. AS THE FIRST OF HIS LABOURS, HERCULES WAS ORDERED BY THE KING OF ARGOLIS TO GO TO NEMEA, DESTROY THE LION AND RESCUE THE PEOPLE. AT FIRST, HERCULES ATTEMPTED TO SHOOT THE LION WITH ARROWS, BUT WHEN THIS TACTIC FAILED, HE THREW HIS WEAPONS AWAY, STRANGLED THE CREATURE WITH HIS BARE HANDS, SKINNED IT WITH ITS OWN CLAWS, THEN CARRIED THE SKIN IN TRIUMPH BACK TO THE KING OF ARGOLIS.

A LEGEND FROM SHINTOISM CONCERNS LEO'S RULING PLANET, THE SUN. AMATERASU, A SOLAR DEITY, WAS FRIGHTENED BY HER BROTHER, THE STORM GOD, AND FLED TO A CAVE, PLUNGING THE WORLD INTO DARKNESS. SHE REFUSED TO COME OUT UNTIL AMA-NO-USUME, THE DAWN GODDESS, CAME UP WITH A PLAN. SHE PLACED A MIRROR NEAR THE ENTRANCE TO THE CAVE AND STOOD NEARBY, EXPOSING HER BREASTS AND PULLING HER SKIRT DOWN. THE GODS LAUGHED SO MUCH THAT AMATERASU BECAME CURIOUS AND CAME OUT. SHE IMMEDIATELY CAUGHT SIGHT OF HER REFLECTION IN THE MIRROR AND WHILE SHE GAZED AT IT, THE GODS GRABBED HER, PULLED HER OUT AND LIGHT RETURNED TO THE WORLD.

IN THE STORY OF HERCULES AND THE NEMEAN LION, THE LION'S DEFEAT IS A SYMBOL OF LEO'S DEEP, OFTEN HIDDEN VULNERABILITY. THE LION ALSO REPRESENTS LEO'S DEEPEST ANXIETIES, FEARS AND EMOTIONAL HURTS. IT CAN ONLY UNDERSTAND AND CONQUER THEM BY FACING UP TO THEM DIRECTLY — IN HAND-TO-HAND COMBAT — A STEP THAT REQUIRES COURAGE AND INSIGHT. THE SHINTO MYTH DEMONSTRATES HOW LEO'S VANITY CAN PROVE TO BE ITS WEAK POINT.

Leo is a noble and generous sign, one that makes the world more pleasurable, creates beauty all around and brings people together in joyful gatherings. Many of the other signs envy it for its self-confidence and courage, and for its ability to get what it wants through a combination of manipulation, willpower, sheer force of personality – and what often looks like good luck. But to Leo, things can seem very different. Sometimes the light of the Sun – Leo's ruler – wanes and Leo's world is enveloped in darkness. Then its appearance of happy-go-lucky bonhomie can be misleading, for Leo is skilled at masking its insecurity and vulnerability. Some people will be fooled, but perceptive friends will realise that Leo is feeling lost and alone, and that it may actually need more support than those who are outwardly less confident.

Being a Fixed sign, Leo's loyalty is one of its best qualities. But the fixed aspect of its personality means that it is also often obstinate and frequently refuses to see the need for change. Complacency – closely linked to resisting change – can be another Leo failing. The sign finds it easy to settle into a comfortable rut, only to be sharply jolted out of it when circumstances alter. What Leo needs is to be able to recognise when it slips into a pointless or self-defeating pattern of behaviour. But since its element is Fire, paradoxically, Leo has a tendency to impulsive and rash behaviour. To counteract this, it must develop the clarity of thought and analytical skills that will help it act in a more measured way.

Leo's ambition is fiery and legendary. But why should it not be so? After all, with the Sun as its ruling planet, the lion as its zodiac symbol and gold as its colour and metal, the sign is traditionally associated with nobility and even with royalty. These Leo symbols regularly appear in coats-of-arms, where they denote the ultimate power

wielded by kings and princes. Leo's ambition also helps to ensure that it has complete faith in itself, which often means that it has a tendency to put its own interests above those of others – not a very attractive characteristic. Sometimes, though, it should tailor its expectations to its skills. It may be surprised to discover that achieving its aims can mean putting in a great deal of effort and not expecting other people to do its work for it.

Leo people are often natural performers: even a quiet, introverted Leo can make a splash on entering a room. They undoubtedly possess a natural stage presence, but just as many actors are actually rather insecure and need audience approval to convince themselves of their own worth, so Leo's loud, flamboyant actions are often calculated to evoke a similar response.

Personalities born with the Sun in Leo include Arnold Schwarzenegger, Mick Jagger, Napoleon Bonaparte, Emily Bronte, Jackie Onassis, Mae West, Lawrence of Arabia, John Logie Baird, Henry Ford and Claude Debussy.

Leo's relationships

Leo's easiest relationships are traditionally with the other Fire signs, Aries and Sagittarius. These all share the belief that life is to be lived, and that there is no point waiting around. When Leo, Aries and Sagittarius want to do something, they get on and do it. If a relationship between Leo and another Fire sign founders, it will be

the lion

LEO'S ANIMAL IS THE LION, KING OF THE JUNGLE, AND A TRADITIONAL EMBLEM OF ROYALTY. AWE-INSPIRING AND FEARSOME, THE LION IS A CREATURE THAT EXUDES POWER AND CONFIDENCE. THE DOWNSIDE OF THIS IS THAT LEO CAN SOMETIMES BE ARROGANT, BOSSY AND OVERBEARING — BUT THIS MAY CONCEAL DEEP-ROOTED UN-LEO-LIKE INSECURITIES.

the sun

JUST LIKE ITS RULING PLANET, THE SUN, WHICH STANDS AT THE CENTRE OF OUR GALAXY AND IS THE SOURCE OF LIFE ON EARTH, LEO LIKES TO BE THE CENTRE OF ATTENTION. AND JUST AS THE SUN HAS BEEN WORSHIPPED THROUGHOUT THE AGES, SO LEO LOVES TO BE ADORED AND APPRECIATED. MOST OF THE SUN GODS OF THE PAST WERE MALE DEITIES, SO IT IS FITTING THAT LEO SHOULD BE A BOLD, ASSERTIVE MASCULINE SIGN. JUNGIAN ASTROLOGERS MIGHT SUGGEST THAT LEO PERSONALITIES NEED TO LOOK CAREFULLY AT THEIR RELATIONSHIP WITH THEIR FATHER TO MAKE SENSE OF THEIR LIVES.

precisely because of what the signs have in common – a desire to be first and a refusal to compromise. But few stages are big enough for two Fire signs, and particularly not for two Leos. For the relationship to succeed, each should take on different responsibilities. Each can shine in his or her own way.

Leo's partnerships with the three Water signs – Cancer, Scorpio and Pisces – also have a fascinating dynamic. Cancer encourages Leo to express itself, so these relationships often take on a dramatic flavour. Meanwhile, Leo is good at dealing with the outer world, while Cancer provides emotional support. Leo and Scorpio are both stubborn, but as long as compatibility is found elsewhere in their charts, harmony between them is likely. But the moment their aspirations and lifestyles take different tracks, they may decide to call it a day. Pisces complements Leo very well, so these relationships can seem made in heaven. Leo's natural mode of operation is open, public and straightforward, while Pisces' is quiet, private and mysterious.

Put Air and Fire together and the result is often explosive. Leo and Gemini can make a perfect, extraordinarily creative match, with Leo providing the enthusiasm and Gemini the ideas. All they require is discipline – and a clear set of goals. Much the same happens when Leo gets together with Aquarius, but in this case, since the attraction can be more compulsive, any irritation between them is that much greater. What these two signs

life-enhancing strategies

- ARE YOU ALWAYS TRYING TO IMPRESS? THIS MAY BE COUNTERPRODUCTIVE AS OTHERS COULD BE ANNOYED BY IT. YOU MIGHT BE HAPPIER IF YOU STOPPED TRYING TO MAKE A SPLASH AND INSTEAD SIMPLY ENJOYED OTHER PEOPLE'S COMPANY. CONCENTRATE ON OTHERS AND YOUR RELATIONSHIPS ARE BOUND TO IMPROVE.

- IT IS ONE THING TO ATTRACT PEOPLE WITH YOUR COLOURFUL PERSONALITY, ANOTHER TO STAY FRIENDS WITH THEM. TO DO SO, YOU MIGHT HAVE TO STOP INSISTING THAT THEY DO WHAT YOU WANT. REMEMBER THAT THEY HAVE NEEDS AND WISHES, AND LIKES AND DISLIKES, WHICH ARE NOT NECESSARILY THE SAME AS YOURS. INSTEAD, FIND OUT WHAT THEY WOULD LIKE AND GO ALONG WITH THAT. THEY WILL BE HAPPY — AND PERHAPS SURPRISED — TO KNOW YOU THINK THEIR VIEWS COUNT.

- DO YOU OFTEN FEEL THAT PEOPLE ARE IGNORING YOU? THE TRUTH IS THAT YOU ARE PROBABLY IGNORING THEM. TRY PUTTING YOUR HURT FEELINGS TO ONE SIDE AND MAKE OTHERS THE CENTRE OF ATTENTION INSTEAD. SURPRISE SOMEONE WHO IS IMPORTANT TO YOU BY SHOWERING HIM OR HER WITH PRAISE AND PERHAPS EVEN WITH PRESENTS.

- YOU LIKE YOUR PARTNER TO LOOK GOOD AND BE SUCCESSFUL IN LIFE, BUT DO NOT RELY TOO MUCH ON THESE EXTERNALS. THEY DON'T LAST FOREVER. INSTEAD, TRY TO REALLY GET TO KNOW THE INNER PERSON.

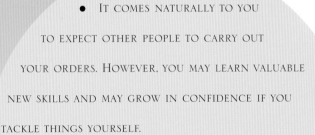

- IT COMES NATURALLY TO YOU TO EXPECT OTHER PEOPLE TO CARRY OUT YOUR ORDERS. HOWEVER, YOU MAY LEARN VALUABLE NEW SKILLS AND MAY GROW IN CONFIDENCE IF YOU TACKLE THINGS YOURSELF.

- IF YOU ARE ATTEMPTING TO FOLLOW A HEALTHIER, FITTER LIFESTYLE, SET YOURSELF SIMPLE, ACHIEVABLE GOALS AND STICK TO THEM. THIS WILL PROVE FAR MORE REWARDING THAN SETTING OUT WITH UNREALISTIC AIMS AND HAVING TO GIVE UP.

need to learn is respect for each other's freedom. As both are concerned with outward appearances, Leo and Libra can be an easier combination. Libra offers Leo almost unlimited support – all Leo needs to do is to repay the compliment and ensure that Libra does not feel ignored.

Leo's relationships with the three Earth signs – Taurus, Virgo and Capricorn – are not considered classically 'compatible' but each has something to offer the other. Earth provides stability, giving Leo a secure base from which it can set off on its creative adventures. Leo may complain about Earth's lack of ambition, but it would do well to recognise that Earth's sound common sense and discipline can be just what Leo needs to achieve its dreams. Leo and Taurus are both stubborn signs, usually convinced that they are in the right. It follows that they will get on wonderfully as long as they agree with one another but, once they do not see eye to eye, their relationship could come to a full stop. Leo and Virgo are very different signs in many respects. They will get along well together provided each has its own distinct responsibilities within the relationship – Leo supplying the glamour and Virgo keeping the everyday details of life running smoothly. Leo and Capricorn have their differences, but Leo's love of luxury complements Capricorn's desire for material wealth. When they come unstuck, Capricorn is alienated by Leo's extravagance, while Leo resents Capricorn's conservative approach to life.

Leo's health and wellbeing

Leo's warm-heartedness and generosity is mirrored in medical astrology for Leo rules the heart. We talk about Leo being 'big-hearted' or, when trying to achieve its aims, determined to go straight to the 'heart of the matter'. To be 'broken-hearted' is to have experienced what, for Leo, is one of the greatest blows – rejection in

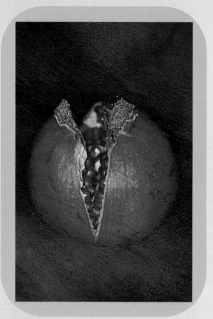

love. Leo's state of health is strongly influenced by its emotional mood. When the sign is up nothing can trouble it; when it is down, it may be prone to all sorts of minor ailments.

The heart, of course, controls the flow of blood, so Leo exercise should aim at improving the circulation. Yogic head and shoulder stands send blood from the feet to the head and make the heart work harder, but Leo people love to win – a gold medal if possible – and yoga is definitely not an activity for competitive spirits. Leo does, though, prefer any exercise that will improve its looks, tighten its stomach or build its muscles, so an ideal gift for a Leo would be a gym membership. Leo can enjoy a session on the weights or the rowing machine, confident that these will improve the heart rate and give a healthy looking body.

Some Leo herbs have a connection to the heart and blood. For example, dandelion is said to cleanse the bloodstream and is rich in vitamins A, B and C. Angelica's connection is more an oblique one: it is said to ease 'heartburn', while the spices turmeric and saffron are traditionally connected to Leo because of their yellow colour.

With its generous nature, Leo is a sign that relishes the pleasures of life. It loves things to look attractive and can be fussy about the way its food is presented. But its weakness is a tendency to excess. While some Leos dedicate themselves to maintaining a young and beautiful appearance, others cannot resist the temptations of food and drink, especially alluring, rich and elaborate cuisines. Some go for both, alternating between binge-eating and crash diets and, of course, this is an unhealthy way to treat one's body. Leo's goal, of course, should be to learn that it is perfectly possible to eat healthy food that also looks appetising.

Hand in hand with Leo's regal attributes goes a love of richness and beauty and it likes to include these, wherever possible, in its surroundings. Hence it is attracted to rich colours, luxurious furnishings and ornate decorations – think elaborate seventeenth-century baroque. Leo also loves strong scents and golden-yellow flowers with large petals – sunflowers and marigolds are perfect. But unfortunately, Leo often sets too much store on appearances and this can make it a bad judge. It needs to work hard to see beneath the surface, to appreciate the real value of something or someone. Once it can do this, its enjoyment of life will be that much greater.

festivals

In Celtic culture, which once spread across
much of Europe, Leo's time of year used to see
the celebration of Lughnasadh – named after Lugh, a
god of light and therefore a Leonine deity. Lughnasadh was
essentially a harvest festival that celebrated in particular the harvesting of
the first corn. Some folklore historians believe that the Lughnasadh celebrations used to include a propitiatory
sacrifice intended to ensure the success of the harvest. The sacrificial victim represented the 'Oak King', a
symbol of the first half of the year. He was killed by burning or was crucified on a cross.

The Buddhist festival of Asala, also known as Dhammacakka or Dharma Day,
meaning 'The Turning of the Wheel of Teaching', is held at the Full Moon
in late July or August. It celebrates the time over two thousand years
ago when Buddha started his teaching of the Middle Way, the Noble
Eightfold Path and the Four Noble Truths. The key feature of Buddha's
teaching – especially relevant in today's must-have society – is that
desire is the root of all suffering. We may not be able to eradicate
desire from our lives, but we can be aware that attainment of those
wishes – particularly material ones – does not always bring happiness.

take a
leaf from leo

LEO LOVES TO PUT ON A SHOW AND SOMETIMES BEHAVES OUTRAGEOUSLY. IF YOU

ARE A RESERVED TYPE YOU MAY FIND THIS SHOCKING, BUT FORCING YOURSELF TO ACT

OUT OF CHARACTER FROM TIME TO TIME CAN BE REFRESHING AND MAY RELEASE EMOTIONS

YOU DID NOT EVEN KNOW YOU HAD. YOU CAN DO THIS IN THE SECURITY OF YOUR OWN

HOME AND HAVE LOTS OF FUN AT THE SAME TIME IF YOU GATHER FRIENDS AND FAMILY

TOGETHER FOR A RIP-ROARING GAME OF CHARADES. LET YOUR HAIR DOWN AND THROW

YOURSELF INTO THE SPIRIT OF THE GAME WITH ALL THE

ENTHUSIASM YOU CAN MUSTER. NOW IT'S

YOUR TURN — LIKE A LEO — TO

TAKE CENTRE STAGE.

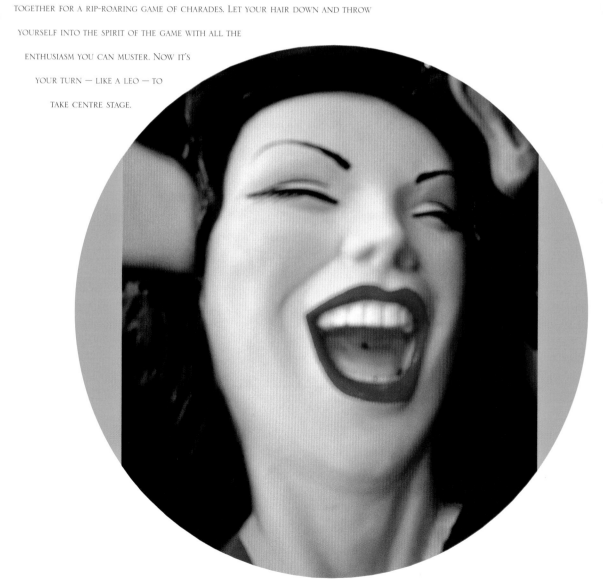

meditation

RULED BY THE SUN, LEO IS A SIGN OF HEAT AND LIGHT. THIS MEDITATION IS DESIGNED TO COUNTER THE DEPRESSING EFFECTS OF COLD AND DAMP THAT LEO CAN FEEL AND TO GENERATE A FEELING OF INNER WARMTH AND WELLBEING. IF IT IS A SUNNY DAY, YOU COULD TRY DOING THIS MEDITATION OUTDOORS.

Lie down or sit in a comfortable chair and close your eyes. Breathe deeply and slowly. Gradually you begin to feel yourself drifting effortlessly away from the ground. You pass through the clouds and into space. You are aware of the Sun in the distance. As you pass through the cold regions of space, your vision is filled with more and more of the Sun's light. Eventually you feel its heat burning your skin. You pass through the surface of the Sun into its

constellation

LEO IS ONE OF THE LARGEST AND MOST INSTANTLY RECOGNISABLE CONSTELLATIONS, PARTLY BECAUSE OF THE SO-CALLED 'SICKLE' OR QUESTION-MARK SHAPE THAT MAKES UP THE LION'S HEAD. THIS UNMISTAKABLE FORMATION RISES OVER THE WESTERN HORIZON SHORTLY AFTER DUSK IN FEBRUARY AND MARCH. ITS BRIGHTEST STAR IS REGULUS, THE ANCIENT PERSIAN 'ROYAL' STAR. THE LION'S BODY TRAILS BEHIND, MARKED BY ABOUT FIVE MAJOR STARS AND ALMOST FIFTY DIMMER ONES. ALTOGETHER, THE STARS OF LEO FORM AS MAGNIFICENT A SIGHT AS ITS ROYAL CONNECTIONS SUGGEST.

regal and imaginative, Leo encourages us to express our creativity

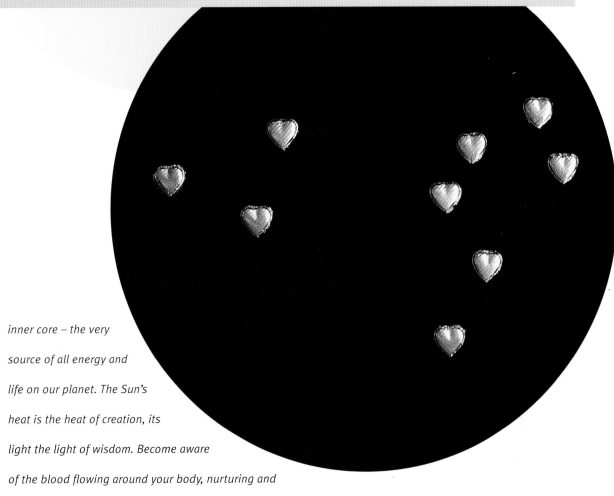

inner core – the very source of all energy and life on our planet. The Sun's heat is the heat of creation, its light the light of wisdom. Become aware of the blood flowing around your body, nurturing and cleansing it. Your body is strong and vital, your mind settled. When you are fully refreshed, you may begin the journey back to Earth. Finally, open your eyes. You will feel revived and full of life and confidence.

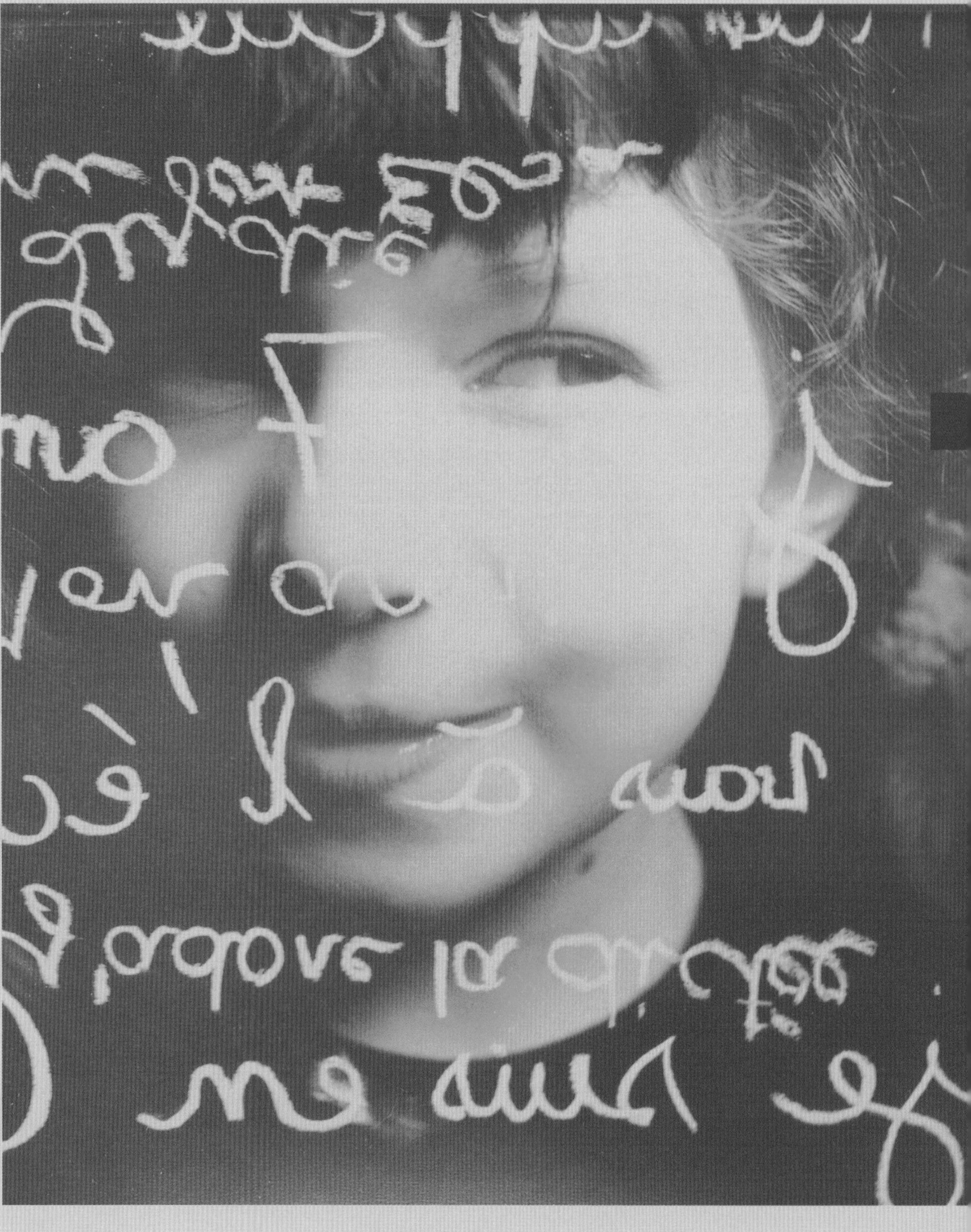

virgo

mutable, earth, female

24 august – 22 september

Virgo is the Great Mother of myth. From her body she brings forth and sustains all life, maintaining order while others create chaos. In Virgo, the earth starts to bear fruit. A sign of dedication and hard work and prepared to put in whatever effort is required to achieve its aims, Virgo also personifies the ability to make choices and to distinguish between right and wrong. Its virtue is its selflessness — while some signs help themselves, Virgo serves others. If Virgo has a fault, it is its tendency to judge both itself and others far too harshly.

For the last two thousand years, the most potent Virgoan symbol has been provided by the Virgin Mary, the mother of Christ. Although she is not strictly a mythological character, the images we have of her with the infant Christ in her arms certainly resemble those of the powerful ancient Egyptian goddess Isis holding the baby Horus — solar deity and child of Osiris the celestial king. Clearly, the Virgin Mary was closely linked in the minds of our ancestors with the great mother goddesses of ancient mythology, such as Isis. In medieval paintings, Mary's close connection with Virgo was depicted by the placing of the star Spica — the star of good fortune from the constellation of Virgo — on her shoulder. While Mary is benevolent, she can also be seen as powerful, able to bear children without a male partner.

Andromeda, the beautiful daughter of Cassiopeia and King Cepheus of Ethiopia, is another Virgoan figure. When Poseidon, god of the oceans, sent a sea monster to ravage Ethiopia, Cepheus and Cassiopeia offered Andromeda as a sacrifice to appease the monster. Happily she was rescued by Perseus, and lived to enjoy a long and virtuous life.

In the Catholic church, the Virgin Mary has come to represent a view of 'the perfect woman'. One problem for Virgoans is their obsession with perfection. They need to accept that neither they nor their friends can ever achieve such a level of perfection. Instead, they should lighten up a little. Andromeda became a sacrificial victim. Virgo must take care not to let itself be exploited and taken advantage of to benefit others.

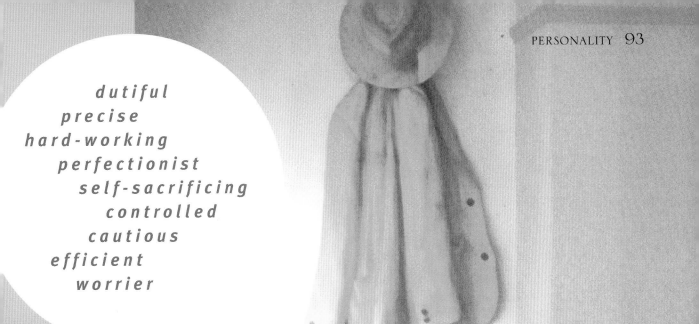

dutiful
precise
hard-working
perfectionist
self-sacrificing
controlled
cautious
efficient
worrier

green, brown, mercury, topaz

Virgo is the second of the Earth signs, the companion to Taurus and Capricorn. Together, these three represent our ability to learn practical tasks, set ourselves goals and achieve results. With Mercury as its ruling planet, Virgo approaches problems in an orderly fashion, first by looking at what it wants to achieve and examining the possibilities, then by setting its priorities and finally by getting on with things. The combination of Earth with the female component of Virgo – as with Taurus – contributes the element of fertility and fruitfulness. This is what, traditionally, links Virgo with ancient mother goddess figures and with Ceres – sometimes used to represent Virgo – the ancient Roman goddess of agriculture. Virgo is also a Mutable sign, and so should be free to change tack at a moment's notice.

Two of Virgo's watchwords are work – if it is not careful, it can easily turn into a workaholic – and duty. Duty is so important to Virgoans that they can sometimes be found doing what they feel they should rather than what they want. Duty is an unfashionable concept in the West nowadays, for everyone is encouraged to do what is right for him- or herself. But the world might be a better place if people took a leaf out of Virgo's book and also actively considered others. And that better, less selfish world is the one that Virgo believes in.

So much emphasis on work and duty can make Virgo a perfectionist and a worrier – characteristics it shares with Cancer. Worrying can, of course, be useful, for people who worry often plan carefully and avoid the pitfalls that catch out their more complacent companions. Fretting only becomes a problem when it paralyses you and prevents you doing anything for fear that something will go wrong. If Virgo recognises this syndrome in itself, it has at least taken the first step towards overcoming it.

mercury

VIRGO SHARES ITS RULING PLANET,
MERCURY, WITH GEMINI, BUT WHEN
MERCURY MEETS VIRGO, THE EMPHASIS IS ON
MERCURY AS THE SYMBOL OF IDEAS AND
INTELLECTUAL ENQUIRY. THIS MEANS VIRGOANS ARE
PEOPLE WHO NOT ONLY GET THINGS DONE, BUT WHO THINK
ANALYTICALLY ABOUT WHAT THEY ARE DOING. THEY ARE
ESPECIALLY GOOD AT DISCIPLINES AND CRAFTS
REQUIRING PRECISION OR CLARITY OF
THOUGHT.

Virgo's perfectionist side has the effect of making it highly critical. Just as its worrying can lead it into total inaction, so its desire for perfection can make it take such a harsh view of its abilities that it ends up attempting nothing. And by seeking perfection all the time, not only from itself but from others, Virgo can end up driving friends and companions away.

It perhaps helps to understand Virgo even more by looking at some of the differences between it and Leo, the sign it follows. Whereas Leo represents raw enthusiasm, the belief that anything can be achieved through sheer willpower, Virgo reminds us that nothing is possible without hard work and dedication, and while Leo tends to look after its own interests, Virgo spends much of its time looking after others. Leo is also a sign that likes to include everyone and everything in its world, extending its largesse and goodwill far and wide. Virgo, on the other hand, is discriminatory and exclusive, selecting some people, beliefs and ideas for its own, and rejecting others. Discrimination is the process by which we decide what is right or wrong, good or bad, safe or dangerous, pleasant or unpleasant, so to have the skill of discrimination is incredibly useful.

Everyone needs a little Virgo in their horoscope, and people who lack this sign's natural caution, practical efficiency and flair for detail would do well to seek out those who have. A Virgoan who perhaps was lacking these last three characteristics was Louis XVI of France, who met an untimely death during the French Revolution, but the sign encompasses a wide range of other famous people, some of whom have more obvious Virgoan traits than others. They include the German poet Goethe and the English writer D.H. Lawrence, as well as Jesse James, Greta Garbo, Mother Teresa, Sophia Loren, Agatha Christie, Sean Connery, Elizabeth I of England and Peter Sellers.

the virgin

VIRGINS HAVE ALWAYS PLAYED A KEY ROLE IN RELIGION AND MYTHOLOGY, USUALLY AS THE INNOCENT WOMAN WHO IS OFFERED AS A SACRIFICE OR WHO DEVOTES HER LIFE TO GOD. IPHIGENIA IN THE ILIAD, THE VESTAL VIRGINS WHO DEDICATED THEMSELVES TO THE GODDESS VESTA AND THE VIRGIN MARY OF THE BIBLE ARE ALL EXAMPLES. MANY VIRGOANS HAVE A PROBLEM EXPRESSING THEIR SEXUAL FEELINGS AND MAY PREFER TO KEEP THEM UNDER CONTROL, RATHER LIKE THESE ANCIENT VIRGINS.

Virgo's relationships

The great gift Virgo brings to all its relationships is its willingness to serve others. As an employee, Virgo is efficient and hard-working and as a friend it is considerate, caring and polite. When in love, it will go to any lengths to see that the object of its affections is happy, but sometimes a line needs to be drawn. Virgo should make sure that it is not exploited and does not sacrifice itself to the point that it turns into a doormat. Sometimes Virgo needs to learn assertiveness, to stand up for itself, speak its mind and simply say no when people make unreasonable demands on it.

Virgoans often do not show their feelings, so are sometimes accused of not having any. This, of course, is not true but they do need to learn to get in touch with their emotions. And while they will probably never indulge in theatrical emotional displays, they would find it liberating to discover appropriate ways of expressing their feelings. In the same vein, Virgoans can also find sexual passions unsettling. They fear that sexual feelings – along with any deep desires – may upset life's order and stability. Yet, as we all know, sexual desire cannot be ignored. Virgo must come to terms with this fact as well as with the feelings themselves.

In their relationships, Virgoan caution can be very useful. It can often save partners from high-risk courses of action, but

life-enhancing strategies

- BEING A PERFECTIONIST CAN MEAN THAT YOU OFTEN REFUSE TO ACCEPT ANYTHING LESS THAN THE BEST — AND END UP WITH NOTHING. SOMETIMES IT MIGHT BE BETTER TO SETTLE FOR SECOND BEST.

- YOU OFTEN FIND THE SHEER FORCE OF YOUR SEXUAL PASSIONS DISTURBING. RATHER THAN TRYING TO SUPPRESS THESE FEELINGS, ENJOY THEM AND TAKE PLEASURE IN YOUR PHYSICAL RELATIONSHIPS.

- IT IS GOOD TO RELY ON THE FACTS FOR SOLVING PROBLEMS, BUT ONCE IN A WHILE, IGNORE WHAT YOUR HEAD TELLS YOU AND FOLLOW YOUR INSTINCT. YOU MAY FIND IT LIBERATING.

- YOU OFTEN HELP OTHERS OUT OF A SENSE OF DUTY, BUT THIS LEAVES YOU OPEN TO EXPLOITATION, SO TRY TO DISTINGUISH BETWEEN PEOPLE WHO GENUINELY NEED YOUR HELP AND THOSE WHO TAKE ADVANTAGE OF YOU.

- IF YOU MUST CRITICISE OTHERS, DO SO CONSTRUCTIVELY AND WITH COMPASSION AND UNDERSTANDING. IF YOU ARE TOO NEGATIVE THEY WILL NOT LISTEN. RATHER THAN TELLING THEM 'DON'T DO THAT', SUGGEST THAT THEY 'TRY DOING IT LIKE THIS'. ALTERNATIVELY, INSTEAD OF SAYING ANYTHING, SET AN EXAMPLE BY YOUR OWN ACTIONS.

sometimes caution turns into fussiness and this can put a great strain on relationships. What Virgo needs is to back off and realise that every detail of life does not have to be planned for things to turn out well.

Virgo's relationships with the Fire signs – Aries, Leo and Sagittarius – gain strength from their differences. Aries' enthusiasm, optimism and spontaneity contrast with Virgo's care, caution and efficiency. Whereas Aries acts as it pleases from moment to moment, Virgo sticks to its long-term plans. If the two people understand their very different approaches, the result can be a productive lifelong partnership, but it is not difficult to see that if they do not, mutual incomprehension and irritation are much more likely. Where Leo is concerned, Virgo's humility can sometimes make a fine match with Leo's egotism, but the relationship may work best when Virgo encourages Leo to take responsibility for everyday, practical affairs and when Leo gives Virgo the support it needs to pursue its deepest ambitions. With Sagittarius, Virgo may be alienated by what it sees as that sign's willingness to take pointless risks and squander everything it has worked for, while Sagittarius will be exasperated by what it sees as Virgo's timidity and lack of imagination. When this happens, Virgo should perhaps remember how much it gains from Sagittarius's willingness to take a gamble, while Sagittarius should never forget the value to the relationship of Virgo's common sense and caution.

Relationships with the Air signs – Gemini, Libra and Aquarius – are based on a similar dynamic, with Air providing the ideas and Virgo the hands-on skills to put them into practice. Virgo and Gemini share a sense of curiosity about the world that can be an excellent recipe for long-term happiness. Virgo and Libra can both be very fussy about their surroundings, so they will have to agree on how everything in the home should be arranged or they will be better off living apart! Virgo and Aquarius have little in common, so any attraction will be an attraction of opposites. If the relationship comes unstuck, Virgo may be irritated by Aquarius's inability to distinguish between what is possible and what is not, while Aquarius wonders why Virgo is so dull.

The three Water signs – Cancer, Scorpio and Pisces – bring emotional depth to a relationship with Virgo. Virgo and Cancer both appreciate domestic security and, having made a commitment, are slow to break it. But they are both worriers, so may seek support and reassurance elsewhere! Virgo and Scorpio can be rather serious characters. Once they are drawn together they will work to see that the relationship endures, but Virgo sometimes finds Scorpio moody, while Scorpio sees Virgo as cold and unfeeling. In a relationship with Pisces, Virgo is entranced by Pisces' deep, romantic dreams, while Pisces relies on Virgo's willingness to deal with the everyday. But when things go wrong, Pisces starts to despise what it sees as Virgo's lack of soul, while Virgo despairs at Pisces' impracticality.

Virgo's relationships with the other Earth signs – Taurus and Capricorn – can be the easiest, for they all agree that actions speak louder than words. Virgo and Taurus may feel an instant rapport and form a lifelong mutually supportive friendship, but it may lack excitement. Virgo and Capricorn are similar; when these get together, they

 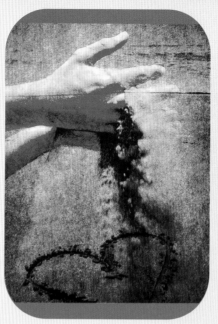 

will do their best to make the relationship work, even if their feelings change. It is in relationships between two Virgos, though, that the truth is faced. Here there is a lack of Fire's enthusiasm, Air's ideas and Water's emotion, so they can drift through life being very busy with small things but failing to make their dreams come true.

Virgo's health and wellbeing

Worry and stress – two of Virgo's main characteristics – can be related to digestive problems, so it is not to be wondered at that in medical astrology, Virgo traditionally rules the stomach. No surprise either then that a number of Virgoan herbs are said to be good for the digestion. Dill is one of these, and so is mint. A glass of mint tea makes the perfect *digestif* after a heavy meal. And since Virgo is traditionally associated with beans – a major cause of flatulence – it is good to know that fennel seed, another Virgoan seasoning, has a reputation for curing the problem.

Through its ruling planet, Mercury, Virgo is also connected to any plant that could be used in magical rituals and divination, or that could induce hallucinations – magic mushrooms and opium come to mind. Perhaps that is why one notable Virgo weakness can be to eat too little and live on stimulants such as cigarettes and coffee. But in general, Virgoans are usually rather health-conscious and are naturally attracted to wholefoods and raw fruits and vegetables. They will prefer organic produce to additive-loaded ready-prepared meals.

Virgo's attitude to health is normally a commonsense one and it tends to steer clear of the latest health fads, so it is more likely to cycle or walk to work or go hiking than spend hours on exercise machines in the gym. Given

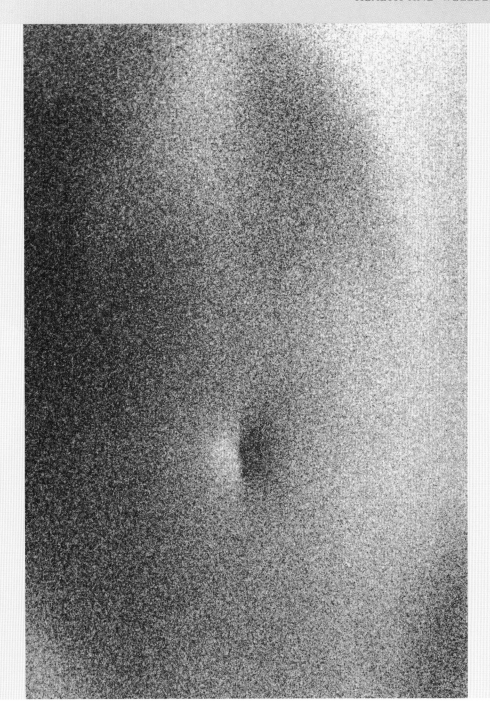

that Virgo hates time-wasting and organises its life down to the last detail, it often gets its exercise while doing something else – gardening, washing the car or decorating the home.

Traditionally, it likes that home to be clean and efficient. An immaculate, futuristic, white-painted computer-run home would suit it down to the ground. If you don't think you can live like that, then steer clear of Virgoans, but if it appeals to you, you can relax in the knowledge that they will probably be happy to keep it clean for you!

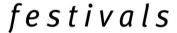

take a leaf from virgo

PEOPLE WHO ARE BORN WITH THE SUN IN VIRGO
LOVE THEIR SURROUNDINGS TO BE CLEAN AND NEAT
AND TIDY. THAT DOES NOT GO FOR EVERYONE THOUGH.
IF YOUR HOME IS IN A PERMANENT STATE OF CHAOS, TRY
HAVING A VIRGOAN TIDY-UP. SET ASIDE A COUPLE OF HOURS
TO SORT OUT YOUR DESK, YOUR WARDROBE, YOUR CAR OR THE
CONTENTS OF YOUR FREEZER. ARRANGE THINGS SO YOU CAN FIND
WHATEVER YOU WANT IN AN INSTANT. IT WILL TRANSFORM
YOUR LIFE. IF THAT'S BEYOND YOU, YOU COULD JUST
TRY CLEANING THE BATH OR YOUR
KITCHEN.

festivals

In the northern hemisphere, this is the time of the harvest. In rural Britain it used to be the custom to make 'corn dollies' – small decorative dolls made of corn stalks. It is thought that these were the descendants of the figurines that used to be made in ancient times to thank the earth goddess for a good harvest. The goddess Ceres, who sometimes represents the sign of Virgo, is depicted carrying a sheaf of corn.

The Jewish new year – Rosh Hashanah – starts just after the new moon in Virgo, as soon as the thin crescent moon can be seen rising in the evening sky. While most Westerners see New Year celebrations as a time to look to the future, Jewish tradition holds that it is also a time to reflect on the past, remember God's purpose in creating the world and ask forgiveness for one's sins. Non-Jews could learn from this: as therapists will tell you, plans for future change rarely work out unless we have come to terms with the past.

At Rosh Hashanah it is customary to eat sweet food such as pieces of apple dipped in honey and honey cake. These symbolise the hope that the New Year will be a sweet and happy one.

Rosh Hashanah is followed by ten days of repentance which climax in Yom Kippur, the Day of Atonement and the holiest day in the Jewish calendar. If Rosh Hashanah is late, Yom Kippur falls after the Sun has moved into Libra. On Yom Kippur, Jews once again ask forgiveness of their sins and resolve to lead a good life in future, an undertaking that is marked by a twenty-five hour fast.

the harvest moon

AN OPTICAL ILLUSION MEANS THAT THE FULL MOON IN
VIRGO OFTEN APPEARS BIGGER THAN USUAL AND ALL AROUND
THE WORLD, THIS FATTER, BRIGHTER MOON HAS BEEN GIVEN A
VARIETY OF DIFFERENT NAMES — HARVEST MOON, FRUIT MOON,
DYING GRASS MOON, BARLEY MOON, SPAWNING SALMON TIME MOON,
CHOKE CHERRIES MOON, ALL RIPE MOON, MOON WHEN PLUMS ARE SCARLET, BIG FEAST MOON —
EVEN SPIDER WEB ON THE GROUND AT DAWN MOON. MANY OF THESE NAMES UNDERLINE THE
CONNECTION BETWEEN VIRGO, FERTILITY AND TIMES OF PLENTY.

a meditation

As an Earth sign, Virgo likes to feel that its feet are firmly on the ground. Yet its rulership by Mercury, the planet of thought, suggests that it can all too easily live in its head and forget to take care of its body. This meditation is designed to remind Virgo — and the rest of us — that we are made of flesh and blood, and that we need to reconnect with the natural world.

If the weather is warm you can do this meditation out of doors. Find a quiet spot to lie down. Watch your breathing and when it becomes slow and regular, begin to think about your body. Become aware of your body as a physical entity. Try to focus on the different parts of your body in turn – your limbs, bones, internal organs. When you feel conscious of your body, begin to think about how you are connected to the material world. Every atom in your body is made from the food you eat, which itself originates in the Earth. Feel at one with the Earth. When you are ready, come back to your body. As you do so, you carry the energy of the Earth with you. You will have a feeling of much greater security and will enjoy the knowledge that the Earth will take care of you.

constellation

VIRGO IS A HUGE CONSTELLATION. ALTHOUGH IT IS NOT ALWAYS EASY TO SEE ITS WHOLE OUTLINE, THE BRIGHTEST STARS SHOULD BE EASY TO SPOT. TO FIND IT, LOOK IN A SOUTH-EASTERLY DIRECTION — NORTH-EASTERLY IF YOU'RE IN THE SOUTHERN HEMISPHERE — LATE IN THE EVENING IN MAY OR JUNE. YOU SHOULD SEE ONE VERY BRIGHT STAR — SPICA, THE STAR WHICH MARKS THE SHOULDER OF THE RECLINING FIGURE OF THE VIRGIN.

detail and practicality show us how to make our dreams come true

libra

cardinal, air, male

23 september – 23 october

At the equinox, on 23 September, day and night are of exactly equal duration, just as they were on 21 March, hence Libra is, above all, a sign of harmony and balance. It weighs up different options, reconciles opposing ideals and goals, and turns conflict and chaos into peace and order. Its strength is its willingness to work hard for a world in which everyone gets on. Its weakness is its inability to make up its mind, but this is counterbalanced by its belief in fairness and justice and its ability to create a harmonious, peaceful environment.

LIBRA'S MYTHOLOGY IS LINKED BOTH WITH ITS SYMBOL — THE BALANCE — AND ITS PLANET — VENUS. OSIRIS WAS THE ANCIENT EGYPTIAN RULER OF THE UNDERWORLD WHOSE SON WAS THE JACKAL-HEADED GOD ANUBIS. ANUBIS ACCOMPANIED OSIRIS ON HIS CONQUEST OF THE WORLD AND, WHEN OSIRIS WAS KILLED, DEVISED THE FUNERAL RITES PRACTISED BY THE ANCIENT EGYPTIANS. THEY BELIEVED THAT A DEAD PERSON WOULD BE LED BY ANUBIS TO THE PRESENCE OF THE DIVINE JUDGES, HEADED BY OSIRIS HIMSELF. WITH DUE CEREMONY, THE DEAD PERSON'S HEART WAS PLACED IN ONE DISH OF A BALANCE WHILE A FEATHER, SYMBOLISING TRUTH, WAS PLACED IN THE OTHER. IF THE HEART WAS LIGHTER THAN THE FEATHER, THE SOUL WAS ADMITTED TO THE REALM OF ETERNAL LIFE; IF HEAVIER, IT WAS CONSUMED BY THE DEVOURER.

FRIJA WAS THE NORSE EQUIVALENT OF VENUS. SHE LOVED RICH JEWELLERY AND ONE DAY COMMITTED ADULTERY IN ORDER TO OBTAIN A GOLDEN NECKLACE. HER SIN WAS DISCOVERED BY HER HUSBAND, ODIN, WHO FORGAVE HER ON CONDITION THAT SHE PROVOKE BLOODY WAR. EACH NIGHT, THE MEN KILLED THE PREVIOUS DAY WERE RESUSCITATED SO THAT THEY MIGHT BE SLAUGHTERED AGAIN THE NEXT.

THE ANUBIS MYTH CLEARLY RELATES TO LIBRA AS A SIGN OF BALANCE AND DECISION-MAKING. ALTHOUGH IT MAY TAKE ITS TIME COMING TO A CONCLUSION, LIBRA WILL ALWAYS WEIGH UP THE PROS AND CONS CAREFULLY, ESPECIALLY WHERE IMPORTANT MATTERS ARE CONCERNED. FRIJA'S GREED IS A WARNING FOR LIBRA. IT SHOWS THE DREADFUL CONSEQUENCES WHEN LOVE OF BEAUTIFUL THINGS — A LIBRAN TRAIT — BECOMES AN OVERRIDING PASSION. THE VIOLENCE THAT FORMS PART OF THE MYTH IS ANATHEMA FOR PEACE-LOVING LIBRA, HENCE THE STORY ACTS AS A DOUBLE WARNING.

diplomatic
charming
controlling
co-operative
level headed
sociable
ordered
strategist
dutiful
polite

white, pastels, copper

Libra is full of contradictions. Together with Aries, Cancer and Capricorn, it is reckoned to be one of the tough Cardinal signs, controlling its environment and influencing events rather than being dominated by them. Yet Libra hates conflict, so to get its own way without confrontation requires a delicate balancing act. It is fortunate then that the sign is so good at reconciling opposites and finding a middle way, qualities that are symbolised by its perfectly balanced scales. In fact it is said that Libra's purpose is to preserve balance and harmony in all things, to achieve peace at any price. The English concept of fair play is often viewed as typically Libran. And with its ruling planet as Venus, the planet of peace as well as the symbol of love and affection, the idea of Libra as a sign that steers clear of conflict is underlined. All this makes it a wonderful example to aggressive, confrontational people and it is not surprising to learn that in a list of professions said to be suitable for Librans, diplomat will always be near the top.

Being an Air sign also makes Libra very good at analysing its feelings – sometimes at the expense of simply experiencing them. But, of course, Librans are human, with hopes, fears, needs and desires like everyone else. Where Libra is different is in that it is often completely out of step with the modern idea that people should be free to do whatever they like whenever they want. It realises that personal feelings sometimes need to be kept in check if everyone is to live and work together happily.

Libra is also renowned for taking its time as it weighs up the pros and cons of a situation, whether it is something as mundane as choosing the best route to a friend's house, or a more significant undertaking such as whether or not to move abroad for the sake of a new job. In such instances, Libra is simply making the most

venus

LIBRA SHARES ITS RULING PLANET, VENUS —
THE BRIGHTEST PLANET IN THE SKY — WITH TAURUS.
WHEN LINKED WITH TAURUS, VENUS'S ATTRIBUTES AS THE
GODDESS OF LOVE ARE DOMINANT, BUT WHEN VENUS IS
ASSOCIATED WITH LIBRA, THE EMPHASIS IS MORE ON VENUS AS
THE GODDESS OF PEACE. THERE IS NOTHING THAT LIBRA LIKES
BETTER THAN TO KEEP THE PEACE AND PROMOTE HARMONY
WHERE THERE IS DISSENT. IF THERE ARE TWO WARRING
PARTIES, YOU CAN RELY ON THIS SIGN TO GET THEM
TO AGREE, CO-OPERATE AND PERHAPS EVEN
LOVE ONE ANOTHER A LITTLE!

of its ability to anticipate the consequences of its actions. It will prepare the ground with meticulous attention to detail before going ahead with anything, but is less concerned with the practical minutiae in a Virgoan sense, than with other people's reactions and with the need to get agreement. As a result, Libra is often accused of indecision. It is one thing to dither over matters of life and death, but Libra can still be mulling over a restaurant menu when its companions have finished their meal. There are moments when Libra can learn from its opposite sign, Aries, and try to be more confident and willing to take the occasional risk.

People born with the Sun in Libra are a very varied bunch. They include Mahatma Gandhi, Margaret Thatcher, John Lennon, Auguste Lumière – the French pioneer of cinematography – Brigitte Bardot, Marie Stopes and the women's tennis champion, Martina Navratilova.

Libra's relationships

Libra is gracious, polite, charming and good company. It is, in short, the sign of partnership. Usually it looks for one special individual to lend it encouragement and support, but often it ends up forming close one-to-one relationships with a series of people.

Because Librans want to get on with everyone and make a point of trying to be liked by all, in their search for friends and partners, they often fall into the trap of refusing to acknowledge irreconcilable differences between themselves and others. For the sake of good relations, they may also find themselves sacrificing their own needs and desires and, because Libra is so concerned with the impression it makes, it sometimes stays in a

the balance

LIBRA'S SIGN — THE BALANCE — IS THE ONLY MECHANICAL, NON-ANIMAL SIGN OF THE ZODIAC. MANY ASTROLOGERS SUGGEST THIS MEANS THAT LIBRANS ARE GOOD AT WEIGHING UP THE PROS AND CONS OF A MATTER WITHOUT LETTING THEIR PERSONAL FEELINGS GET IN THE WAY. OTHERS GO FURTHER, SAYING THAT LIBRANS ARE SIMPLY COLD, UNEMOTIONAL TYPES.

relationship for the sake of appearances. This is behaviour that was once the norm and won universal approval, but now it has rather fallen out of fashion.

As an Air sign, Libra lives in the world of ideas, so is often trying to make sense of its relationships instead of simply enjoying them. It tends to enter a relationship full of preconceived notions about the other person and about what a relationship should consist of. That is fine if its partner fits the mould, but there will be problems if Libra tries to change him or her to fit its tidy and ordered view of things. In Libra's universe, emotions can be messy things, causing all sorts of unpredictable traumas and upsets, yet to be a fully rounded person, Libra needs to learn to get in touch with its feelings and experience the heights and depths of human passion.

Libra's relationships with the three Earth signs – Taurus, Virgo and Capricorn – are not normally described as compatible, but this is to overlook the qualities that each sign gives the other, and especially the fact that the Earth signs provide Libra with stability and security. Libra and Taurus share a love of beauty, which can make it easy for them to agree on how they decorate their home, and they can also get on well on a professional level. Libra and Virgo, meanwhile, are both perfectionists, always striving for a better world. If they share the same goals and acknowledge that they might not always see eye to eye, they can have an extremely positive relationship, but when they clash, it can be very difficult for them to find any common ground. When Libra gets together with Capricorn, the relationship can work very well, for Capricorn puts Libra's ideas into practice while Libra provides the social skills that Capricorn may lack.

life-enhancing strategies

- You often feel as if you are under pressure from others to come to a decision. Rather than make a hurried choice, explain that you need more time. If a deadline is looming, write down the pros and cons of each possible choice, considering the likely consequences — the risks as well as the benefits — of any particular course of action. This should clarify your thoughts and help you reach a decision.

- You owe it to yourself to keep your surroundings peaceful and beautiful. If the people you live with bring clutter and noise into the home, at least try to preserve a clean, airy, quiet space that is for you and you alone.

- Creating peace and harmony makes you feel good. You enjoy knowing you have done your bit for a better world. But if you are struggling to right a wrong or resolve a conflict and are not meeting with success, think whether it is worth the effort. Perhaps it is better to leave others to sort out their own problems just this once.

- Are you bottling up your feelings for someone? If so, write your feelings down on a piece of paper and try to find a way of telling the person how you feel.

- Stop worrying that people may not like you. It is not necessary for everyone you meet to be your friend.

Libra always does its best to get on with everyone, even with the impatient and impetuous Fire signs, Aries, Leo and Sagittarius, whose harsh, abrasive edge it often succeeds in softening. The relationship between Aries and Libra can be close and when it is, these two form something akin to a mutual admiration society. Aries is charmed by Libra's softness while Libra is thrilled by Aries' ruthlessness. When they fall out, Aries is infuriated by Libra's indecision while Libra is dismayed at Aries' aggression. Libra and Leo share a love of pleasure, although Librans may not like it when Leo goes a bit wild. Libra and Sagittarius may travel the world together, but there may come a time when Libra wants to 'do the right thing' while Sagittarius yearns to follow its fancy.

The three Water signs – Cancer, Scorpio and Pisces – are often attracted to Libra's air of level-headed calm. With their tempestuous emotions they imagine that Libra can handle anything. They also think that Libra knows all there is to know about relationships. Libra, meanwhile, is excited by the Water signs' intensity but if trouble strikes, it will find Water immature and overemotional. Libra and Cancer share the ambition and desire for a better life that comes with being Cardinal signs but as they both like to be in control, there is a risk of disagreement when they live together. When Libra is with Scorpio, Libra's willingness to gloss over uncomfortable feelings often collides with Scorpio's desire to challenge taboos and bring hidden passions to the surface. Libra and Pisces often make the best partnership because both like to keep up appearances and avoid unpleasantness.

When it comes to the Air signs, Libra's relationships with other Librans are often marked by a deep empathy and a determination to get on well, but sometimes they lack excitement and spontaneity. They exchange ideas and agree on what must be done, but never do it! Libra and Gemini can strike up a very friendly rapport, although Libra can find Gemini too scatty and disorganised, while Gemini objects to the fact that it thinks Libra is always telling it what to do. Libra and Aquarius often also recognise each other as soul mates, but Libra's need for certainty can clash with Aquarius's belief that it has the right to do whatever it chooses.

Libra's health and wellbeing

In medical astrology Libra rules the kidneys. These play an important role in cleansing the body of toxins and a number of key Libra-associated plants are said to help with this process. One is thyme, which is also an antiseptic, a second is dandelion, which also has a reputation for easing rheumatism, gout and stiff joints, while

a third is horseradish, which is said to stimulate the glandular system into throwing off poisons, thus assisting the kidneys in their work. Libra, as a sign of balance, is also in tune with the concept of Yin and Yang, the two complementary principles of Chinese philosophy. Their interaction is thought to maintain the harmony of the universe and to influence everything in it. The goal of the Chinese practices of Feng Shui and acupuncture is to try to achieve a balance between Yin and Yang in ourselves and our environment.

Signs such as Pisces and Taurus flourish in a tranquil environment, but for Libra to keep healthy, peace is paramount. Any hint of conflict brings a rapid rise in Libra's stress levels and when it feels tense, almost any complaint can be exacerbated. It is no surprise then that Libra's ideal environment is clean and uncluttered. It likes its home to be decorated with matching colours and furnishings and it prefers calming white and pastel shades. Whenever it can, it will add a touch of class with tasteful objects and works of art. In fact, one characteristic of Librans is their ability to create pleasing surroundings. It is as though they are born interior designers, with an innate sense of what looks good together.

When it comes to keeping fit, Libra does not like to suffer, so it is rare for it to be keen on participating in rough competitive sports. According to some astrologers, the game of cricket, with its complicated rules of etiquette and its sparkling white clothes, is a classically Libran sport. The analogy could be extended to squash and tennis – both ball games played in pleasant surroundings – and to the genteel game of croquet. But, with its concern for appearances, Libra is frequently attracted to exercises that will, for example, tone the stomach muscles rather than promote overall good health.

And because Librans are so concerned with appearances, they tend to work hard at making the most of their own. In this they are usually successful. Their style of dress is quiet and attractive. They try not to be noticed, but may draw attention to themselves precisely because they are so well turned out. Sometimes they can be too concerned about appearances and should, perhaps, be more prepared just to be themselves instead of worrying what others think. If you are the partner of a Libran you can look forward to a calm, stress-free existence, but just once in while, you might yearn for Libra to let go, relax and live a little.

take a leaf from libra

Is there something you have been putting off doing,
some decision you have avoided making? Indecision and
procrastination affect us all, so take this opportunity to
deal with any problem that has been hanging over you.
Libra is renowned for its skill in weighing up an
argument, so follow its example and review all
the pros and cons carefully. It
always pays to see all sides
of an issue.

festivals

The most renowned Libran festival, that of
the Greater Eleusinian Mysteries, took place in
ancient Greece at Eleusis, a sacred site not far from Athens. It
began on 23 September, the time of the autumn equinox and one of the moments of balance in the Sun's
journey. Around the year 360 A.D., the Roman emperor Julian wrote his Hymn to Cybele, the Mother of the
Gods, in which he stated that 'the Goddess herself chose as her province the cycle of the Equinox. For the
most sacred and secret Mysteries are celebrated when the Sun is in the sign of Libra'. The Mysteries involved
rituals, processions and offerings to the goddess. The remission of sins was a central goal of the festival and
its key myth was that of the abduction of Kore (Persephone to the ancient Greeks, Proserpina to the Romans)

to the underworld
by Hades, its king, and her subsequent
release. This myth symbolises the 'darkness' that descends
on the earth in winter – Libra falls as the nights start to lengthen. It is
also a variant of the 'dying god' myths in which human beings acknowledge
that death must come before rebirth, that there can be no dawn without night and no
seed until after the harvest.

In modern times, Libra sees moon-harvest festivals celebrated in Vietnam and China. In Vietnam, the full moon in the eighth lunar month, usually in late September in the West, is the excuse for the Tet Trung Thu harvest festival. Children, representing faith in the future, figure prominently. They parade through the streets, carrying elaborate lanterns and singing and beating gongs and drums. They are given presents of toys and candied fruit and eat a special cake in the shape of a half-moon – banh trung thu.

At the Chinese moon-harvest festival, moon cakes often contain hard-boiled duck-egg yolks that are intended to represent the moon. The children sing a delightful song which translates roughly as, 'It's now mid-autumn and the moon is round. Grandpa is making the moon cakes for me. Moon cake is round, sweet and delicious. One piece of moon cake, one of heart.'

as the sign of the balance, Libra encourages fair play,

a meditation

LIBRA IS THE SIGN OF COLLABORATION WITH OTHERS, AND ITS POSITION IN THE BIRTH
CHART INDICATES THE AREA OF LIFE WHERE WE ARE LIKELY TO SEEK PARTNERS, SEARCH FOR
CO-OPERATION AND WORK FOR PEACE. THIS MEDITATION IS DESIGNED TO HELP US UNDERSTAND
OUR RELATIONSHIPS AND WHAT WE NEED FROM OTHER PEOPLE.

*Find a quiet place to lie down, relax, close your eyes and breathe deeply and calmly. When your mind is still,
think of someone who is very important to you. It could be someone from your present or your past, a friend,
family member, lover, teacher, work colleague – anyone. Imagine yourself and this person standing, facing each
other, perfectly still. What is it about the other person that you like? Is this a characteristic that you wish to have
yourself? Imagine your body and mind merging with theirs. Feel as if you are taking on their strengths. Those
things that they can do, you can do too. When you open your eyes, you will feel more confident, less dependent
on others and better able to control your own life.*

constellation

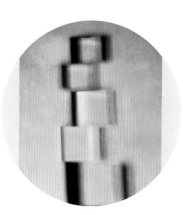

THE EASIEST WAY TO SEE LIBRA IS TO FIND VIRGO THEN LOOK
ALONG TO THE LEFT (TO THE RIGHT IF YOU ARE IN THE SOUTHERN
HEMISPHERE) TO THE NEXT MAJOR GROUP OF STARS. THIS IS THE CONSTELLATION
OF LIBRA. ITS TWO BRIGHTEST STARS ARE ZUBANELGENUBI (ARABIC FOR 'SOUTHERN
CLAW') AND ZUBANESCHAMALI ('NORTHERN CLAW'), FROM WHICH THE TWO BALANCES
OF THE SCALES HANG. THESE NAMES SUGGEST THAT LIBRA MAY ONCE HAVE BEEN PART
OF SCORPIO. ZUBANESCHAMALI IS THE LOWER OF THE TWO STARS AND IS SUPPOSED TO
BE THE ONLY GREEN STAR IN THE SKY. THE FACT THAT NOBODY CAN MAKE UP THEIR
MIND ABOUT THIS IS PERHAPS A REFLECTION OF LIBRAN INDECISION.

justice and respect for different beliefs and opinions

scorpio

fixed, water, female

24 october – 22 november

SCORPIO IS A DEEP, DARK, MYSTERIOUS SIGN, RENOWNED FOR ITS INTENSITY AND PASSIONS. IT TAKES US INTO THE HIDDEN REALMS OF INTUITION AND INSTINCT AND IS THE BRIDGE BETWEEN THIS WORLD AND THE NEXT, BETWEEN BODY AND SPIRIT, MATTER AND ENERGY. THE SIGN OF THE HEALER AND SKILLED AT TREATING EMOTIONAL WOUNDS, SCORPIO ALSO REPRESENTS REGENERATION AND REBIRTH. ITS WEAKNESS IS ITS READINESS TO BEAR A GRUDGE AND SEEK REVENGE, BUT ITS STRENGTHS ARE ITS LOYALTY TO ITS FRIENDS AND ITS WILLINGNESS TO HELP THOSE IN NEED. ITS SENSE OF JUSTICE AND RIGHTEOUSNESS ARE SECOND TO NONE, BUT IT SOMETIMES JUDGES OTHERS TOO HARSHLY.

The most awesome Scorpio creatures in mythology are the Scorpion-men in the Epic of Gilgamesh. Gilgamesh — a solar hero and Mesopotamian king — is on a journey that mirrors that of the Sun as it travels through the year. Gilgamesh meets the terrifying Scorpion-men who guard the mountain that protects the Sun. They question him on the reasons for his journey and he reveals that he wishes to understand the secrets of life and death and come to terms with a bereavement he has suffered. Deciding that this is a noble quest, the Scorpion-men permit Gilagamesh to pass on his way, but he has to travel in darkness. Finally Gilgamesh arrives at his journey's end. Here the sun is shining and there is a bright new dawn.

Another Scorpionic legend concerns Hercules and the Lernean Hydra. The hydra, a monster with many heads, lived in a Scorpionic cavern in the middle of the stinking swamp of Lerna. Hercules' task was to kill the hydra, but every time he cut off one of its heads, two more grew in its place. Finally, Hercules entered the cavern carrying a blazing torch, which killed the hydra with its brightness.

Mythological journeys are said to represent the gaining of self-awareness, and since Scorpio is a sign that is supposed to be adept at understanding people, it is appropriate that the Scorpion-men should help Gilgamesh during his journey. The Lernean hydra is believed to represent our inner fears. They can only be overcome when we shed light on them. This is a useful message for Scorpio, which has a tendency to keep its feelings secret.

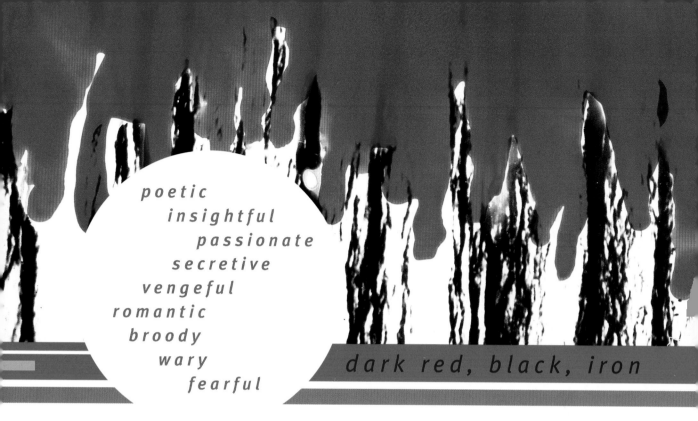

poetic
insightful
passionate
secretive
vengeful
romantic
broody
wary
fearful

dark red, black, iron

Scorpio's ruling planet is energetic, assertive Mars, but as one of the Water signs, it is also sensitive and emotional, responding to events as its feelings dictate and pursuing goals according to its desires and passions. Together with Taurus, Leo and Aquarius, it is a Fixed sign, so like them it is loyal, faithful and capable of undying love, but the downside of this is that it can be obstinate and unwilling to change, so while Scorpio is known for being a devoted friend and companion, it can sometimes get stuck in a rut. What it needs to learn is to be more flexible, more willing to compromise, more ready to see others' points of view and, like Cancer, to be more prepared to let go of the past.

Scorpio's symbol is the scorpion, a creature with a sting in its tail that spends much of its life hiding under stones and in cracks in rocks. Many classic Scorpio occupations are linked with the sign's secretiveness. They include the job of the spy, who must operate covertly without being caught, and that of the detective, whose task it is to catch criminals by learning their secrets. Scorpio is also considered a fine sign for priests, part of whose job is to listen to people's secrets, and for psychologists, who have to analyse and explain them.

But the scorpion's tendency to live in quiet, dark places, and its sting, are in fact both protective measures, and so it is with Scorpio. It is not dishonesty or a desire to deceive that drive the sign to keep its emotions and actions secret, but a lack of confidence, for Scorpio fears criticism and always prefers to steer clear of conflict. It will resolve any obstacles by working away at them until they finally give way or, like its fellow Water signs, Cancer and Pisces, by the simple trick of going around them. If Scorpio is to achieve its ambitions, it would rather do so without confrontation.

mars & pluto

SCORPIO SHARES ITS RULING PLANET, MARS, WITH ARIES. MARS WAS ORIGINALLY A GOD OF FERTILITY AND AGRICULTURE AND SO CAME TO BE ASSOCIATED WITH SEXUALITY AND, ESPECIALLY, MALE POTENCY. FROM THIS COMES THE IDEA THAT SCORPIO IS A 'SEXY' SIGN, BUT PERHAPS IT WOULD BE BETTER TO CALL IT A PASSIONATE SIGN, FOR SCORPIO PEOPLE ARE RENOWNED FOR THEIR INTENSE PASSIONS — EVEN IF THEY KEEP THEM HIDDEN AWAY MOST OF THE TIME. THE PLANET PLUTO WAS DISCOVERED IN 1930 AND IS THE FARTHEST KNOWN PLANET FROM THE SUN. THIS MAKES IT SOMETHING OF A MYSTERY — JUST LIKE SCORPIO.

Similarly with its emotional life. Scorpio's intense emotions are legendary but, so skilled is the sign at concealing its feelings, people often assume it is lacking in emotion. The truth is very different though, for in fact, Scorpio can often feel worn out after the roller-coaster ride its emotions take it on, sometimes in the course of a single day. When it gives the impression of being cold or frosty, it is simply throwing a protective barrier around itself. At times it fears that as soon as it expresses one feeling, all the rest will pour out in an unstoppable torrent and then it is afraid of the reactions this will provoke in others.

Perhaps because it is so familiar with difficult emotions, Scorpio is regarded as a sign of healing, particularly emotional or spiritual healing. It is said to be a sign that harbours deep hurts and so is well equipped to understand other people's wounds. Counselling, therapy and psychiatry are all regarded as professions that are ideal for Scorpio, but the sign is at its best when it is offering advice to loved ones. It listens carefully, empathises well and is good at offering well-considered and insightful solutions.

If Scorpio is to get a better press, more attention needs to be focused on its reliability and less on its supposedly devious qualities. For when Scorpio finds something it believes in, whether that is its friendships, its work or its children, it will do whatever it can, through thick and thin and regardless of the cost or personal risk, to support that something. This makes Scorpio a true friend, a trustworthy employee and a caring parent. In addition, Scorpio has a great sense of humour – possibly becaue it understands that some of life's problems are best dealt with by laughing them away!

People who were born with the Sun in the sign of Scorpio include Pablo Picasso, Rock Hudson, Marie Curie, Indira Gandhi, Marie Antoinette, Hillary Clinton, Cleo Laine, Roseanne, Tatum O'Neal, Prince Charles, Vivien Leigh, Charles de Gaulle, Richard Burton, Demi Moore, Leonardo di Caprio, the Brazilian football player, Pele, and the poets Dylan Thomas, John Keats and Sylvia Plath.

Scorpio's relationships

To enter into a relationship with such an emotionally intense, extremist sign as Scorpio can be overwhelming. It will almost certainly be an experience to remember. For a start, Scorpio is sometimes described as a sensual sign, an association that probably stems as much from the fact that in medical astrology Scorpio rules the reproductive organs as from the sign's passionate nature. In fact, Scorpio often struggles with its passions, wondering if it should pursue its desires whatever the risks, or instead lead a safe and uneventful life.

But to see how Scorpio manages its relationships, it is more useful to look at its scorpion symbol. Dark, mysterious Scorpio finds it very difficult to talk about its feelings. Even when it wants to, it sometimes has trouble finding the right words. Not surprisingly, misunderstandings occur and when Scorpio doesn't say what is on its mind, partners will often come

life-enhancing strategies

- As a Fixed sign, you have a tendency to develop rigid ideas that can lead you into dogmatic thinking about people, politics and religion. Try to be aware of this and open your mind to other possibilities.

- If a relationship leaves you feeling hurt or rejected, you often withdraw into your Scorpionic hole and try to avoid future relationships. But one bad experience does not mean that all relationships are bad. Try to trust people again and learn to open up.

- You are entitled to keep your secrets, but remember that if you don't let other people know what you are feeling, you can't complain when they misunderstand you.

- Is there something you have been longing to say to someone? Try to find the best possible way to say it and if you are nervous, start by trying it out on a friend, to give you confidence.

- You often harbour grudges and that is not always to your advantage as it can cut you off unnecessarily from someone. If a person offends you, ask yourself if they really meant to do so. If you come to the conclusion that they did not, try to put the grudge behind you.

- Your actions in the present are often based on feelings that are stuck in the past. Be aware of this tendency, otherwise what you do now might be determined by events that have nothing to do with your current circumstances.

- Just because your sun sign is Scorpio does not mean that you have the right to deceive people or take revenge on anyone you feel has wronged you.

- Remember that you are not the only sensitive person in the world. If someone close to you is upset, try to be first on the scene offering support and comfort.

to the wrong conclusions, sometimes with disastrous results. There is no doubt that Scorpio can help by making a conscious effort to be more open.

Scorpio also has a reputation for being jealous and possessive, but that is not necessarily because it thinks it owns other people or believes it has the right to control them. The reason is that Scorpio – like Cancer (scorpions and crabs both have claws!) – hates change, so will try to hang on to a relationship even when it is really over. Pulling out the stops to make a relationship work and to try to get through a difficult period is admirable, but Scorpio sometimes needs to recognise that it is time to move on.

Scorpio's relationships with the three Air signs – Gemini, Libra and Aquarius – are marked by the collision between raw Scorpionic passion and the Air signs' belief in the importance of facts. When trouble occurs, the Air signs think everything would be all right if only everyone would sit down and be reasonable, while Scorpio believes that everyone should simply follow his or her feelings. It is no surprise that these signs can often talk at cross-purposes, but when relationships between them work, Air is fascinated by Scorpio's hidden depths,

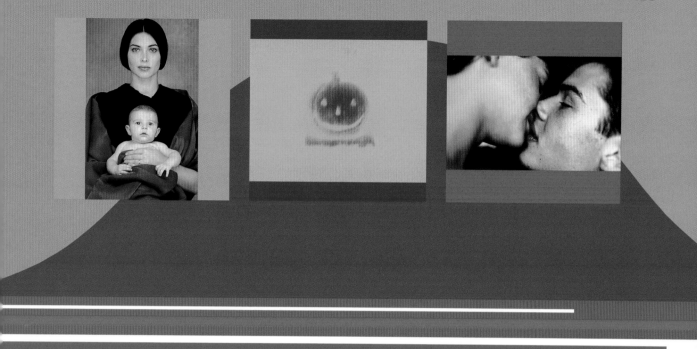

while Scorpio finds Air's clear, rational approach deeply refreshing. Scorpio and Gemini are a strange mixture, but get on as long as Scorpio is happy for Gemini to talk about everything and Gemini is content for Scorpio to talk about nothing! Scorpio and Libra have a perfectionist streak in common, but Scorpio can find Libra superficial and Libra may accuse Scorpio of being moody. Scorpio and Aquarius can be a perfect pair as long as they share the same ambitions, but their stubbornness can cause major disagreement over even tiny details.

Relationships with the three Fire signs – Aries, Leo and Sagittarius – can be passionate when they share the same goals, but if Scorpio's aims, objectives and opinions differ from Fire's, the result may be frustration and incomprehension. Scorpio's determination to get its way secretively can also clash with Fire's desire to make its ambitions public. Scorpio and Aries could not be more different; Aries is open and direct while Scorpio is secretive and complicated, yet both are determined. If they agree on their goals, they can have a productive and enduring relationship. Scorpio and Leo can get on if they share the same objectives, but the slightest falling out can be a major problem for often – as with Scorpio and Aquarius – both refuse to compromise. In addition, Scorpio can be irritated by Leo's dramatisation of small problems, while Leo sometimes cannot cope with Scorpio's brooding. Scorpio's friendships with Sagittarius are based on the attraction of opposites; these work as long as each respects the other's independence.

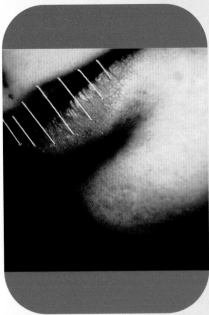

The Earth signs bring stability, material security and protection from mundane pressures to Scorpio, leaving Scorpio free to deal with its complex inner life. Taurus and Scorpio's relationship can be among the closest in the zodiac but if they fall out, Taurus is bemused by Scorpio's intensity, while Scorpio despairs at what it sees as Taurus's failure to experience real feelings. Scorpio and Virgo share a desire to work for a better world and both combine efficiency with emotional commitment, yet Virgo can see Scorpio as sulky, while Scorpio thinks that Virgo lacks empathy. Scorpio and Capricorn are both said to have good business skills, which augurs well for professional relationships, yet Scorpio's willingness to express its emotions – negative as well as positive – is at odds with Capricorn's reluctance to show its feelings and its tendency to put business first.

Relationships with Cancer and Pisces – fellow Water signs – are the simplest. Scorpio and Cancer often become firm allies, finding a deep bond in their romantic view of the world, yet sometimes they are so similar that they begin to seek excitement elsewhere. Scorpio and Pisces can form a really strong relationship, especially when Pisces gets a kick out of Scorpio's intensity and Scorpio benefits from Pisces' ability to make light of life's little problems. When two Scorpios get together, either both have an instinctive understanding of the other's deepest desires, or they keep their feelings so secret that there is no chance of any meaningful communication.

Scorpio's health and wellbeing

In medical astrology Scorpio rules the reproductive and excretory organs. This makes it (like Taurus) a sign of fertility and (like Libra) a sign of cleansing. Some of the plants that are traditionally associated with Scorpio are also linked to these organs. Raspberry leaf, taken as a tea, is said to be very useful for minor problems arising

from pregnancy and childbirth. Chicory is a Scorpionic diuretic, while elderberry, which can be used to make wine, is both a diuretic and is reputed to soothe burns and scalds. Scorpio's mineral salt, calcium sulphate, is considered an excellent purifier that aids the elimination of waste from the body. It can also be found in onion, garlic, leeks and mustard – all of which are linked to Scorpio through Mars, Scorpio's ruling planet.

Scorpio is something of an extremist, so needs to learn moderation. It is likely to indulge in rich food and alcohol, then to swing to the other extreme and follow an excessively restrictive diet. It can take a long time to discover the virtues of healthy eating, but once it has, it is very fussy, checking ingredients in food products to avoid artificial additives and turning its back on chips and buns in favour of brown rice and wholemeal bread.

Regular exercise is important for working off the emotional tension that Scorpio builds up. Any vigorous activity is particularly recommended for working off Scorpionic frustrations, but the traditional combat sports like boxing and wrestling may appeal to Scorpio's martial nature. In general, Scorpio loves to win and hates to be a loser, so may well only take part in competitive sports if it is pretty sure it is going to be successful.

In the home, Scorpio's preference is, like the scorpion's, for an environment that is secure, quiet – and often dark. The colours traditionally associated with it are dark red and black and it loves to be surrounded by mysterious knickknacks and objects from its distant past. If you are living with a Scorpio you may well wish that just occasionally, it would throw open the windows and let in some light and fresh air.

take a leaf from scorpio

SCORPIO IS ASSOCIATED WITH DEATH AND REBIRTH. EVEN IF YOU ARE NOT A CATHOLIC CELEBRATING ALL SOULS' DAY, THIS IS A TIME OF YEAR TO REMEMBER FRIENDS AND FAMILY WHO HAVE PASSED ON. PRIVATE RITUALS OFTEN HELP WITH COMING TO TERMS WITH LOSS OR GRIEF. TRY REVISITING PLACES THAT HAVE ASSOCIATIONS WITH THE DEAD PERSON OR MAKE A LITTLE SHRINE AT HOME, DECORATED WITH A PHOTOGRAPH OF THE LOVED ONE AND PERHAPS A VASE OF THEIR FAVOURITE FLOWERS. AS YOU PASS BY, REMEMBER ALL THE GOOD TIMES YOU SPENT TOGETHER.

festivals

As a sign of darkness and mystery, Scorpio, not surprisingly, is associated with death and the afterlife and a number of festivals celebrated at this time of year share that association. All Saints' Day, originally known as All Martyrs or All Hallows, is celebrated on 1 November. It is a day when Catholics offer thanks for the lives and work of all the dead saints, especially those who do not have their own special day. The evening before – the evening of 31 October – is All Hallow's Eve, or Halloween as it is now commonly known. Heavily coloured by modern American practices, Halloween often involves children dressing up in ghoulish masks, knocking on people's doors and asking for a 'trick or treat'. The biggest Halloween parade in the world takes place in New York, where more than half a million people watch each year as thousands of revellers in fancy dress march through the city. Such theatrical or humorous festivities have the power to neutralise our fear of death.

All Souls' Day, 2 November, is a day in the Catholic calendar for remembering dead loved ones. In Mexico, it is known as the Day of the Dead and the celebrations are rather gruesome, but very colourful. They start on 31 October when the souls of dead children (*angelitos*, or 'little angels') return to earth. On 1 November, peals of church bells welcome the adult souls. People set up altars in the corners of their homes and decorate them with offerings to the dead of fruit, special types of bread, skulls and skeletons made from sugar, paper cut-outs and photographs of the dead. On 2 November, relatives fast and visit the cemetery, taking flowers – fresh or paper ones

hot pursuit

AN AUSTRALIAN ABORIGINAL TALE EXPLAINS THE FORMATION
OF THE CONSTELLATION OF SCORPIO AND HAS ASSOCIATIONS WITH
SCORPIO'S REPUTATION AS A SYMBOL OF SEXUALITY. IT RECOUNTS HOW A
BOY WHO WAS BEING INITIATED INTO MANHOOD WAS SEDUCED BY A YOUNG
GIRL. WHEN THE COUPLE WERE DISCOVERED, THEY ESCAPED INTO THE SKY, PURSUED
BY THE BOY'S TEACHERS WIELDING THEIR BOOMERANGS. ALL OF THEM BECAME THE
STARS OF SCORPIO, WHILE THE BOY'S HEADBAND, WHICH HE LOST DURING HIS
FLIGHT AND WHICH SYMBOLISES HIS FAILURE TO COMPLETE HIS INITIATION, IS
THE STAR CLUSTER JUST BELOW THE CONSTELLATION. IT IS SAID THAT HE IS
FOREVER TRYING TO RECOVER THE HEADBAND, BUT IS HELD BACK BY HIS
LOVER. AND SO HE IS PUNISHED FOR BREAKING THE LAW WHICH
FORBIDS A NEWLY INITIATED MAN FROM HAVING SEXUAL
RELATIONS WITH A WOMAN UNTIL THE INITIATION
CEREMONY IS COMPLETE.

– candles and incense to decorate the graves. Sometimes paths of petals are laid out from the cemetery to the house to enable the dead to find their way from their graves back to their homes.

Often when the Sun is in Scorpio in the Western zodiac, Hindus celebrate the festival of Diwali. This is in honour of Lakshmi, the beautiful goddess of wealth and prosperity. The name means 'festival of lights' from the custom of hanging little clay lamps, or divas, symbolising good fortune, in windows or outside the house. Divas are also placed in small boats of leaves or coconut shells, and are carried downstream or out to sea. People dress in their best clothes, visit family and friends, clean and decorate their houses, make offerings in the temple, send greetings cards, share their food and give trays of sweets as presents. The festival also marks a new business year, a time for paying debts, settling accounts and starting new ventures.

a meditation

BEING A SIGN OF INTENSE EMOTIONS, SCORPIO CAN OFTEN BE TROUBLED BY FEARS IT DOES NOT REALLY UNDERSTAND. THIS MEDITATION IS BASED ON DREAM THERAPISTS' THINKING, THAT WHEN WE ARE TROUBLED BY DEEP, HALF-UNDERSTOOD FEARS, WE FIRST NEED TO LEARN MORE ABOUT OURSELVES. ONCE WE HAVE DONE THIS, WE WILL BE ABLE TO KNOW OUR FEARS BETTER AND SO CONFRONT THEM. THROUGH GREATER SELF-KNOWLEDGE, OUR FEARS WILL APPEAR LESS THREATENING.

Find somewhere quiet to lie down. Make sure that the light is low. Relax and watch your breathing until it is slow and regular. If it helps, play some quiet, gentle music. Imagine that you are walking along a beach. The air is cool, the water calm. You arrive at a cave. You wonder what is inside. You enter cautiously. As you go inside, you sense that there is some presence deep in the cave that is making you feel uncomfortable. What can it be? You keep walking but as you get closer, you realise that the presence is yourself. Greet it. Talk to it. Ask it what it wants. In so doing, you will learn what your deepest wants and needs are. When you are ready, return to the daylight. When you open your eyes, you will feel happier and more aware. You will know that your deep fears can be faced and resolved. They will no longer hold you back as they did before.

constellation

THE CONSTELLATION OF SCORPIO IS ALWAYS KNOWN AS SCORPIUS
TO DISTINGUISH IT FROM THE ASTROLOGICAL SIGN. THE EASIEST WAY TO
FIND IT IS IN JULY, WHEN IT RISES AFTER DUSK. FIRST LOOK FOR THE REDDISH STAR
ANTARES — THE 'HEART' OF THE SCORPION. THIS IS THE BRIGHTEST STAR IN THE WEST
(AS LONG AS THERE ARE NO PLANETS AROUND). THE 'HEAD' OF THE SCORPION IS FORMED BY
BRIGHT STARS TO THE UPPER RIGHT (LOWER LEFT IF YOU'RE IN THE SOUTHERN HEMISPHERE)
OF ANTARES, WHILE THE SCORPION'S 'TAIL' IS A LINE OF STILL MORE BRIGHT STARS STRETCHING
AWAY TO THE LEFT (TO THE RIGHT IN THE SOUTHERN HEMISPHERE).

that are deep, hidden, emotional, loyal and profoundly idealistic

sagittarius

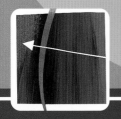

mutable, fire, male

23 november – 20 december

SAGITTARIUS IS AN ADVENTURER, A WANDERER, A FREE SPIRIT WHO SOARS WITH THE CLOUDS AND REACHES NEW HEIGHTS. IT IS THE ARCHETYPAL EXPLORER, CHARACTERISED BY ENERGY, ENTHUSIASM AND FAITH IN THE FUTURE. ITS STRENGTH IS ITS LOVE OF LIBERTY AND ITS WILLINGNESS TO EXPLORE ALTERNATIVES, WHETHER EMOTIONAL, PHYSICAL, INTELLECTUAL OR SPIRITUAL. ITS WEAKNESSES ARE ITS TENDENCY TO TAKE REFUGE IN DOGMA AND ITS LACK OF CONSISTENCY. ITS COMMITMENT TO THE TRUTH IS ADMIRABLE, ESPECIALLY WHEN IT SEES THAT KNOWLEDGE OF THE FACTS IS NOTHING WITHOUT TRUE WISDOM.

ONE OF THE MOST IMPORTANT SAGITTARIAN MYTHS IS THE ANCIENT GREEK STORY OF THE BATTLE BETWEEN THE LAPITHS AND THE CENTAURS. THE CENTAURS WERE GENERALLY GROSS, BARBARIC AND RUDE. PEIRITHOUS, KING OF THE LAPITHS, MADE THE MISTAKE OF INVITING THE CENTAUR EURYTION TO HIS WEDDING. PREDICTABLY EURYTION GOT FIGHTING DRUNK AND TRIED TO ABDUCT THE BRIDE. HE WAS STOPPED BY THESEUS AND THROWN OUT OF THE WEDDING FEAST, BUT RETURNED WITH A GANG OF CENTAURS ARMED WITH SLABS OF STONE AND PINE TRUNKS. THERE WAS FIERCE FIGHTING BUT THE LAPITHS EVENTUALLY WON.

ANOTHER SAGITTARIAN MYTH COMES FROM THE LOUCHEUX PEOPLE OF CANADA. THEY TELL OF A BOY WHO WAS ALWAYS USING MAGIC TO GET WHAT HE WANTED. AT NIGHT, HE WOULD WATCH THE MOON AND SEE HOW IT CHANGED SHAPE AS IT MOVED THROUGH THE SKY. HE ADMIRED IT SO MUCH THAT HE WISHED HE WERE ON THE MOON. HIS MAGIC PROVED SO STRONG THAT HE SHOT UP AND OUT THROUGH THE CHIMNEY. AS HE WENT, HIS TROUSER LEG WAS TORN OFF. AND NOW, WHEN THE FULL MOON RISES, THE BOY CAN BE SEEN STANDING ON THE SURFACE OF THE MOON WITH HIS BARE LEG — OR SAGITTARIAN THIGH — FOR ALL TO SEE.

NO-ONE WOULD DARE SUGGEST THAT SAGITTARIANS BEHAVE LIKE CENTAURS, BUT SOME ASTROLOGERS BELIEVE THAT THE LINK COMES THROUGH THE WORD 'CENTAUR', WHICH CAN MEAN 'THOSE WHO ROUND UP BULLS'. THUS A CENTAUR WAS AN ANCIENT COWBOY — A HERO WHO GOES WHERE HE WANTS AND REFUSES TO BE TIED DOWN — A TYPICAL SAGITTARIAN. THE LOUCHEUX STORY SHOWS SAGITTARIUS AS A SEEKER OF KNOWLEDGE AND SOMEONE WHO ALWAYS WANTS TO BE SOMEWHERE ELSE.

explorer
changeable
independent
discoverer
philosophical
dogmatic
risk-taking
religious
free spirit

fiery oranges, purple, tin

Sagittarius is the sign of freedom and, as the third of the Fire signs, possesses great reserves of enthusiasm, optimism, energy, initiative and generosity. It has an intuitive eye for possibilities that escape other people, and often looks to faraway places or distant cultures for inspiration. It is impulsive, rash, likes to try its luck and is often willing to take a risk. It is not a sign that is happy being told what to do, but neither does it necessarily want to give orders. Sagittarius is also one of the four Mutable signs, so needs to be able to feel free to change course at a moment's notice and follow paths that may lead far from the beaten track.

Its zodiacal animal is the centaur, a mythical creature with the body of a horse but a human head and torso. It is thus one of the dual signs (like the half-goat, half-fish Capricorn) whose nature features a clash of opposites – the rational, civilised human being versus the instinctive animal. Centaurs were generally wild creatures, but one, Chiron, was noted for his wisdom. This side of the centaur leads modern astrologers to observe that the sign has access to higher knowledge, that it represents the sage, the prophet, the teacher and the philosopher, hence its association with universities and churches, lawyers and priests. Nowadays, the animal side of Sagittarius lies largely buried, while the human, civilised side prevails, but both still exist in Sagittarius's personality. That must be why Sagittarius can be both preacher and libertine, spending half its time in communion with the gods, half in debauchery – just like Jupiter, its ruling planet.

Also critical to Sagittarius's nature is the fact that its centaur symbol is depicted as an archer. Astrologers talk of how the sign flies like an arrow, but never reaches its target – hence Sagittarius is a wanderer or nomad, and is constantly searching for knowledge, learning new things, updating itself on the latest goings-on in the world.

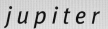

jupiter

SAGITTARIUS'S RULING PLANET, JUPITER, IS
THE GREAT GAS GIANT OF THE SOLAR SYSTEM. ITS
MASSIVE GRAVITY FIELD ACTS LIKE A GIANT VACUUM
CLEANER, SUCKING IN COMETS AND OTHER DEBRIS. THE
ROMAN GOD JUPITER WAS THE KING OF HEAVEN BUT, LIKE
SAGITTARIUS'S CENTAUR, HE HAD A DOUBLE NATURE. WHEN
HE WAS NOT DISPENSING WISDOM AND JUSTICE, HE WAS
SEDUCING WOMEN. THIS FREEDOM TO DO WHATEVER
ONE WANTS IS TYPICAL OF SAGITTARIUS'S
ADVENTUROUS CHARACTER.

When it comes to religious beliefs, the
nomadic Sagittarius becomes a seeker after truth,
a spiritual traveller whose journey never finishes. As
an intellectual, Sagittarius always asks awkward questions
and, as a Mutable sign, it is prone to radically changing its opinions, so
if it starts out as a devout believer, it is likely that at some point in its life it will question all its old assumptions
and become an atheist. But, as Sagittarius teaches us – it is more important to travel than to arrive.

Sagittarian Sun sign people, past and present, include the following: Imran Khan, Jimi Hendrix, Alexander
Solzhenitsyn, Mary Queen of Scots, Jane Austen, Hector Berlioz, Winston Churchill, Kim Basinger, Maria Callas,
Louisa May Alcott, Bette Midler, Arthur Conan Doyle, Paul Getty, Walt Disney and Tina Turner.

Sagittarius's relationships

Being a wandering, independent spirit, Sagittarius has less need for relationships than most other signs.
But it is also very sociable, and if that sounds like a contradiction, then it is! It loves company and has many
friends, but it is not that interested in tying itself down to just a few close friendships or to one romantic
commitment. Not surprisingly then, Sagittarius can be maddening to live with and anyone who enters into a
close relationship with this sign must do so full of respect for its right to preserve its independence. The last
way to treat Sagittarius is to try to pin it down or expect it to make lifelong commitments. The challenge for
Sagittarius in a relationship is to develop emotional intimacy without sacrificing its freedom.

the archer-centaur

SAGITTARIUS'S ZODIACAL SIGN IS THE ARCHER-CENTAUR.
THE ARCHER REPRESENTS THE WANDERING, SEEKING SIDE OF
SAGITTARIUS THAT IS APPARENT IN ITS PASSION FOR LEARNING
AND ITS DESIRE TO STRIKE OUT ON ITS OWN. THE CENTAURS
OF MYTHOLOGY WERE GENERALLY WILD, LECHEROUS
CREATURES, BUT THERE WERE SOME WHO WERE
WISE AND THOUGHTFUL. SO, WHEN IT COMES
TO SAGITTARIANS, IT'S NOT MUCH USE
EXPECTING CONSISTENCY.

Part of this intimacy consists of understanding and respecting other people's feelings and realising that it is as important to recognise others' need for freedom as it is to fight for one's own. It also consists of learning to acknowledge stormy emotions rather than denying them, and of facing up to crises instead of walking away from them. Like its fellow Fire signs, Sagittarius sometimes has a tendency to blame other people for holding it back. Often, though, it is Sagittarius that is looking for an excuse not to press ahead. A partner provides a handy scapegoat.

Cautious signs, such as the Earth signs, Taurus, Virgo and Capricorn, can gain a great deal from a relationship with Sagittarius. Taurus, for example, learns that it is all right to take risks occasionally. Meanwhile Sagittarius can behave in an even more unpredictable manner than usual, secure in the knowledge that Taurus will keep things secure on the home front. Sagittarius and Virgo are both Mutable signs, so their relationships may be marked by a willingness to chop and change and muddle through. Yet there may come a time when Sagittarius wants to spread its wings, while Virgo wishes to stay put, and then the two may have to part. Sagittarius is adept at encouraging Capricorn to question its beliefs, change its habits and generally be more adventurous. If the relationship breaks down, Capricorn often takes offence at the way in which Sagittarius appears to squander its opportunities and refuse to take anything seriously, while Sagittarius finds Capricorn impossibly dull.

Sagittarian relationships with the Water signs can be affectionate, for Scorpio, Pisces and Cancer are all thrilled by Sagittarius's open-hearted generosity and courage, while Sagittarius is enchanted by Water's romantic imagination. Sagittarius and Scorpio provide the strangest combination because the former is honest and direct,

life-enhancing
strategies

- TO HAVE YOUR OWN IDEAS AND OPINIONS TAKES A GREAT DEAL OF EFFORT, SO SOMETIMES IT SEEMS EASIER FOR YOU TO ACCEPT A SET OF PREJUDICES AND PASS THEM OFF AS YOUR OWN BELIEFS. REMEMBER THAT FOR SAGITTARIUS, WISDOM INVOLVES KEEPING AN OPEN MIND.

- YOU CAN BE IMPULSIVE AND SOMETIMES FAIL TO STICK TO THE GOALS YOU SET YOURSELF. TO KEEP ON COURSE, SET YOURSELF A SERIES OF TARGETS, WITH A DEADLINE FOR EACH. THAT WAY YOU ARE MORE LIKELY TO ACHIEVE YOUR GOAL.

- YOU HAVE A TENDENCY TO WALK OUT ON A RELATIONSHIP IF YOU FEEL YOUR PARTNER IS TRYING TO PIN YOU DOWN OR HOLD YOU BACK. BUT IS THIS REALLY WHAT IS GOING ON OR ARE YOU USING IT AS AN EXCUSE FOR NOT ACHIEVING YOUR AIMS? IF THAT IS THE CASE, START PUTTING SOME EFFORT INTO ACHIEVING WHAT YOU WANT INSTEAD OF BLAMING SOMEONE ELSE FOR YOUR FAILURES.

- AS A SAGITTARIAN YOUR DREAMS ARE OFTEN BIG ONES, SOMETIMES TOO BIG TO COME TRUE. BE REALISTIC ABOUT WHAT IS ACHIEVABLE.

- YOU OFTEN IMAGINE THE GRASS IS GREENER SOMEWHERE ELSE. BUT IS IT REALLY? TRY LOOKING AT ALL THE GOOD THINGS ABOUT YOUR LIFE AND MAKE THE MOST OF THOSE RATHER THAN DREAMING OF ESCAPE.

- NOTHING CAN TAME YOUR SAGITTARIAN SPIRIT, SO THERE'S NO NEED TO SEE EMOTIONAL COMMITMENT AS NECESSARILY LIMITING OTHER FREEDOMS. IF YOU FIND IT DIFFICULT TO COMMIT, CONSIDER WHY. PERHAPS IT HAS NOTHING TO DO WITH YOUR CURRENT RELATIONSHIP.

the latter secretive and indirect. Like many relationships between so-called incompatible signs, they can get along famously as long as they acknowledge their differences and make the most of them. Sagittarius and Pisces can be a particularly creative combination, one that augurs well for an enduring friendship. Cancer, meanwhile, can provide Sagittarius with emotional security – when it wants it – although it can fail to understand Sagittarius's need to take off at a moment's notice. When these relationships come unstuck, Sagittarius no longer feels that it can do what it wants, while Cancer, Scorpio and Pisces just cannot take the pace.

When the Air signs – Gemini, Libra and Aquarius – meet fiery Sagittarius the results can be explosive. These relationships tend to flare up without warning, but can burn themselves out if they are not sustained by Earth's stability. For example, when Gemini and Sagittarius get together, Gemini brings its plans, ideas and dreams, while Sagittarius provides enthusiasm and a vision of the future. Sagittarius and Libra share a mutual creativity and idealism, and if they are on the same wavelength can achieve much together. If they drift apart, it may simply be that each has found different interests and their lifestyles just start to diverge. The combination of Sagittarius and Aquarius is perfect for wanderers and for those with no desire for a permanent home and

the wounded healer

JUPITER IS NOT THE ONLY CELESTIAL BODY LINKED TO SAGITTARIUS. IN 1977 THE FIRST OF A NEW CLASS OF ASTEROID WAS DISCOVERED AND WAS NAMED CHIRON AFTER THE WISE CENTAUR. ASTROLOGERS HAVE TAGGED CHIRON 'THE WOUNDED HEALER' AND HAVE DEVELOPED HOROSCOPE INTERPRETATIONS BASED ON THE IDEA THAT THE ASTEROID REPRESENTS WOUNDS WE HAVE TO HEAL, TRAUMAS WE MUST OVERCOME AND DIFFICULT LESSONS WE NEED TO LEARN.

with little inclination to work for worldly success or wealth. If they get stuck with professional commitments and family responsibilities though, each has to find a way of sacrificing some of its freedom – not always the easiest of tasks for these signs.

When it comes to the Fire signs, relationships with Aries and Leo are considered classically compatible since all share an energetic and assertive approach to life. However, if their opinions and goals differ fundamentally, they will go their own way, for once they disagree, they often find it impossible to compromise. Two Sagittarians together either feel an instant rapport, each admiring in the other the qualities they value in themselves, or take an instant dislike to each other, hating in the other those things that they find embarrassing or uncomfortable in themselves.

Sagittarius's health and wellbeing

In medical astrology Sagittarius rules the thighs, while Jupiter, the sign's ruling planet, is linked to the liver, the main organ of the body associated with detoxification and the breakdown of fat. With its link to the thighs and its love of freedom, Sagittarius's classic forms of exercise are walking and jogging while, like Gemini, its opposite sign, Sagittarius finds that running is a great way of working off any nervous energy. As far as team sports are concerned, Sagittarius can take them or leave them. It finds it fun to be part of a team sometimes, but if it thinks of something it would rather be doing, it will simply fail to turn up for practice sessions and will soon be out of the team. It won't care, though, because it will already be off somewhere else, having the time of its life.

One or two Sagittarian plants are closely linked to aspects of the sign's health. Chicory is said to aid the smooth functioning of the liver, while dandelion, which also relieves aches and pains, is reputed to cleanse the system, especially the liver, gall bladder, spleen, kidney and urinary tract.

Sagittarius's eating habits are usually adventurous and always changeable. It may pass through a vegetarian phase, then spend time as a vegan, and finally decide that what it really needs is a juicy, rare steak at least once a day. If it decides to lose weight, the chances are it will go on a severely restrictive crash diet and shed the pounds very quickly, but then it will lose interest and go back to its old eating habits.

The ideal Sagittarian environment should reflect the sign's need for freedom. It likes to live in spacious, open surroundings, decorated with beautiful, uplifting objects yet free of clutter. It is not a hoarder and will happily clear out its wardrobes and cupboards every so often and start again. Unfortunately, if you are a hoarder and live with a Sagittarian, you may come home one day to find that all your treasured possessions have been taken to the charity shop. But sometimes, Sagittarius does not notice its surroundings at all. That can be because it has its mind on higher things or because it is not planning to stay around for long!

take a leaf from sagittarius

IS THERE SOMEWHERE YOU HAVE ALWAYS LONGED TO VISIT? HAVE YOU BEEN HELD BACK BY FAMILY COMMITMENTS, LACK OF MONEY, LACK OF TIME? OR IS THERE SOME SKILL YOU HAVE ALWAYS WANTED TO LEARN, SUCH AS SWIMMING OR SNOWBOARDING, PLAYING A MUSICAL INSTRUMENT, SPEAKING A FOREIGN LANGUAGE? LET THIS BE THE YEAR WHEN YOU MAKE ONE OF THOSE DREAMS COME TRUE.

festivals

The most notable festival to take place at this time of year is the Jewish eight-day festival of Hanukkah, or Festival of Lights. Because the Jews follow a lunar calendar, Hanukkah can fall either when the Sun is in Sagittarius or when it is in Capricorn. The festival commemorates the rededication of the Temple in Jerusalem, after the Jews were liberated from their Greek rulers in 165 B.C. Its celebration of freedom is thoroughly Sagittarian. During the period of the Greek conquest, the Temple was captured and its 'eternal flame' was extinguished. When the Jews, under the leadership of Judas Maccabeus,

recaptured Jerusalem, they
found that there was only one
day's supply of the holy oil needed for the
flame. A messenger was sent to get some more but the journey there and back took eight days. Miraculously,
the oil lasted the whole eight days. Today, during the festival of Hanukkah, as well as giving small presents
on each day to the children of the household, it is the custom to light candles – one on the first day, two on
the second, and so on until the room is ablaze with the light of eight candles.

Sagittarius brings one other major festival – Thanksgiving, celebrated in the United States of America on
the fourth Thursday in November. The traditional Thanksgiving meal consists of turkey, cranberry sauce and
pumpkin pie. Thanksgiving commemorates the survival and first harvest of the settlers who left England for
America. At the end of their first year, they gave thanks to God and ate a celebratory meal to which they
invited the native Indians who had given them food when they were in danger of starvation.

144

the Sagittarius in us all encourages us to be a wanderer,

a meditation

SAGITTARIUS IS THE SIGN OF UNRESTRICTED FREEDOM, YET IT IS A CONDITION OF NORMAL LIFE THAT ONE'S FREEDOM IS RESTRICTED, WHETHER BY FAMILY RESPONSIBILITIES, FINANCIAL CONSTRAINTS, SOCIAL TABOOS OR THE INEVITABILITY OF ILLNESS AND AGEING. THIS MEDITATION IS DESIGNED TO RECAPTURE THE FEELING OF FREEDOM THAT ENABLES SAGITTARIUS TO LIVE ITS LIFE MORE POSITIVELY.

Find a spacious place to lie down or sit if that is more comfortable. Close your eyes and relax. Imagine yourself in a wide open space, like a prairie. The normal pressures of life have disappeared. The sun is high in the sky and the warm breeze on your face induces a feeling of contentment. You slowly realise you are free. You can run to the horizon, fly and travel wherever you want, even to other galaxies. How does that you make you feel? From outer space you can look back to Earth. See how small it looks. Your spirit is much bigger. When you are ready, open your eyes and return to the world knowing that no obstacle or limitation can truly stand in your way.

constellation

SAGITTARIUS IS THE FIFTEENTH LARGEST CONSTELLATION AND INCLUDES MORE THAN SIXTY-FIVE VISIBLE STARS. THE BRIGHTEST OF THESE LINK UP TO FORM WHAT MANY PEOPLE SEE AS A 'TEAPOT', ALTHOUGH OTHERS SAY IT RESEMBLES THE OUTLINE OF A SAILING BOAT. NO DOUBT, THOUGH, OUR ANCESTORS CLEARLY SAW A CENTAUR! TO FIND THE CONSTELLATION, LOCATE ANTARES, THE UNMISTAKEABLE RED STAR IN SCORPIO. THEN LOOK TO THE LEFT (TO THE RIGHT IF YOU'RE IN THE SOUTHERN HEMISPHERE) AND THE NEXT GROUP OF STARS WILL BE SAGITTARIUS.

an explorer, a philosopher and a lover of freedom

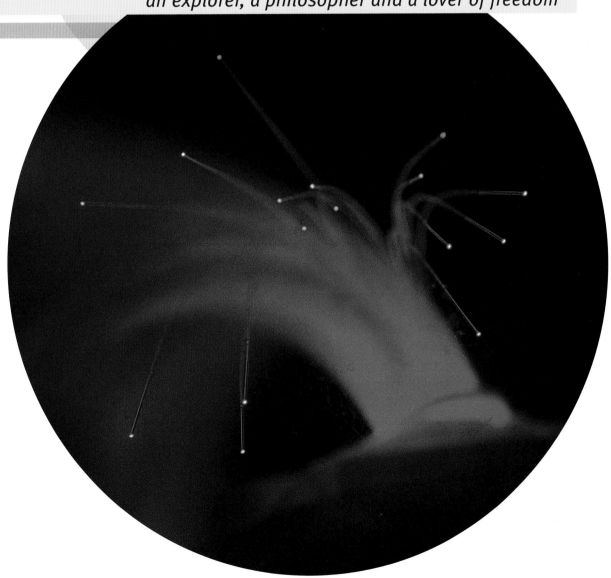

capricorn

cardinal, earth, female

21 december – 20 january

IN CAPRICORN, THE SUN DIES AND IS REBORN. THE WINTER SOLSTICE ON 21 DECEMBER BRINGS THE LONGEST NIGHT AND THE SHORTEST DAY. FOR A MOMENT THE SUN APPEARS TO STAND STILL. ALL IS CALM BEFORE IT ENTERS THE NEXT PHASE OF ITS ZODIAC JOURNEY. CAPRICORN'S STRENGTHS ARE ITS DEVOTION TO DUTY, ITS WILLINGNESS TO FULFIL ITS RESPONSIBILITIES AND ITS ABILITY TO PROVIDE ORDER, STABILITY AND MATERIAL SECURITY. ITS WEAKNESSES ARE ITS CONSERVATISM AND UNWILLINGNESS TO TAKE RISKS. BUSINESS SKILLS COME NATURALLY TO CAPRICORN, BUT IT IS A GREATER CHALLENGE IF IT IS TO EXPLORE ITS EMOTIONS. CAPRICORN'S DEEPER TASK IS TO EXPLORE THE REALMS OF THE SPIRIT.

SOME OF THE RICHEST OF ALL ASTRAL MYTHOLOGY SURROUNDS CAPRICORN'S RULING PLANET, SATURN, KNOWN TO THE ANCIENT GREEKS AS CRONOS. THE ANCIENT LEGENDS TELL US HOW CRONOS ROSE UP AND OVERTHREW HIS FATHER, URANUS, THE SKY GOD. IN TURN, CRONOS WAS OVERTHROWN BY HIS SON, ZEUS, AND IT WAS FURTHER PROPHESIED THAT ZEUS WOULD BE REPLACED BY APOLLO, THE SAVIOUR OF THE WORLD. AS EARLY CHRISTIANS NOTED, SOME OF THE TEXTS WHICH FORECAST APOLLO'S COMING BORE A PROFOUND RESEMBLANCE TO JEWISH PROPHECIES OF THE MESSIAH.

IN ADDITION, THE ANCIENT GREEK POET HESIOD TELLS US THAT CRONOS WAS THE RULER OF A LEGENDARY GOLDEN AGE WHEN THE WORLD WAS HAPPY, HEALTHY AND PEACEFUL. IT WAS PARTLY THIS THAT PROMPTED AUGUSTUS, THE FIRST ROMAN EMPEROR, TO PUT CAPRICORN'S GOAT-FISH ON A SERIES OF COINS MINTED DURING HIS REIGN, SENDING THE MESSAGE THAT THIS WAS THE START OF A NEW GOLDEN AGE. CRONOS MAY BE COMPARED TO THE JUDAEO-CHRISTIAN GOD OF THE BIBLE, RULING OVER THE PARADISE-LIKE GARDEN OF EDEN. CRONOS IS ALSO, THEREFORE, A SYMBOL OF UNATTAINABLE IDEALS, FOR THOUGH WE MAY LONG FOR THOSE DAYS TO RETURN, WE KNOW THEY NEVER CAN.

CAPRICORN IS A SIGN THAT SETS A GREAT DEAL OF STORE ON WEALTH AND STATUS. WHAT THE SUCCESSION OF RULERS IN THE URANUS-CRONOS-ZEUS-APOLLO STORY TELLS CAPRICORN IS THAT ALL THINGS MUST PASS, THAT HOWEVER GREAT ONE BECOMES, WE ALL RETURN TO DUST. CAPRICORN IS ALSO INTENSELY CONSERVATIVE. IT HARBOURS MEMORIES OF A GOLDEN AGE WHEN LIFE WAS BETTER AND GIVEN THE CHANCE, WILL OFFER ITS OPINION THAT SOCIETY IS GOING DOWNHILL.

thoughtful
practical
conservative
earthy
stable
serious
intense
dutiful
shy

browns, lead

Capricorn is a rich and versatile sign, capable of springing many surprises on those people who assume that it is cautious, businesslike, practical, unimaginative, unromantic, reluctant to express passion – in short, dull. But a quick look at its symbolism reveals that this is a one-dimensional view. For a start, the Sun is in Capricorn at one of the most sacred points of the year in both the Christian and the pagan calendars. Pagans celebrate the rebirth of the Sun, the symbol of life; Christians the birth of Christ, the bringer of salvation. From this one might deduce that Capricorn possesses more depths than some of the other signs, not less.

As it happens, Capricorn's feelings are as intense as any other sign's. It is just that, as an Earth sign, it always keeps an eye on reality, seeing what it can actually achieve and being conscious of the fact that there are always practical considerations to be taken into account to make a dream come true. With this in mind, Capricorn does not waste its time on unrealistic projects and does not usually stick around people who do.

Capricorn is also one of the four Cardinal signs, so it likes to control its environment rather than be dominated by it. It might achieve this through a career in business, politics or even organised religion. Its approach tends to be conservative, holding on to what is familiar and taking few risks. This may not be a quality that appeals to impatient people, but it can be valuable and can save Capricorn and others from making careless mistakes.

Capricorn's ability to work hard and do its duty often brings it success and status – attributes the sign strives for. However, it must avoid looking for excuses such as financial considerations or social disapproval – both of which may not be relevant anyway – in order not to take any risks.

saturn

CAPRICORN'S RULING PLANET,
SATURN, IS SAID TO BE A PLANET OF
HARD WORK AND OBSTACLES, BUT IT ALSO
INDICATES STATUS AND HONOUR, REWARDS
EFFORT AND HAS NO TIME FOR QUICK FIXES.
CAPRICORNIANS ARE NOT AFRAID OF HARD
WORK AND ENJOY ANY PRESTIGE THEY ACHIEVE
AS A RESULT. BUT THEY SHOULD REMEMBER NOT
TO ALLOW THIS TO BECOME THE BE-ALL AND
END-ALL OF THEIR EXISTENCE.

The hardworking, dutiful and responsible sides of Capricorn's personality are attributes that receive a poor press in today's society, where it is all right for people to follow their feelings no matter what the consequences. But Capricorn is most comfortable when it is working hard, earning the respect of the community and developing a sense of belonging. Like Cancer, its opposite sign, Capricorn likes to feel part of a close-knit group or of a circle of friends, but whereas Cancer looks for emotional security, Capricorn often seeks material security first.

Capricorn can boast of a wide variety of personalities born when the Sun is in its sign. These include Elvis Presley, Aristotle Onassis, Louis Pasteur, Janis Joplin, Simone de Beauvoir, Joan Baez, Henri Matisse, Mao Tse Tung, Nostradamus, Fay Dunaway, Martin Luther King, Marlene Dietrich and J. Edgar Hoover.

Capricorn's relationships

When it comes to mixing with others, the typical Capricorn is polite and good mannered, so he or she will know whether, on meeting someone, it is appropriate to shake hands or to offer one kiss on the cheek or two. Not surprisingly, then, Capricorn favours a traditional approach to relationships and one of its admirable qualities is that, influenced by what it thinks is best for its partner and its children, as well by what other people think, it will usually do the 'right thing'. If a relationship hits a rocky patch, Capricorn will work hard to do whatever is necessary to see that it survives and will often be the last to walk out when the going gets tough.

Young Capricorns are frequently attracted to people who are older, wiser or more experienced, partners who have already sown their wild oats and are ready to settle down. Being rather conservative, a Capricorn may well

the goat-fish

CAPRICORN'S SIGN IS A GOAT, OCCASIONALLY SHOWN WITH A FISH'S TAIL. THE FISH SYMBOLISES EMOTIONAL DEPTH, ARTISTIC IMAGINATION AND DREAMS. THERE ARE TWO TYPES OF GOAT — THE DOMESTIC ANIMAL TETHERED TO ITS POST AND THE MOUNTAIN GOAT LEAPING FROM CRAG TO CRAG. A GOAT WHO IS DEDICATED TO ACQUIRING MONEY AND STATUS AT THE EXPENSE OF ITS FEELINGS MAY END UP EMPTY INSIDE, WHILE THE ONE WHO PUTS IMAGINATION FIRST CAN CREATE CHAOS IN ITS PRACTICAL AFFAIRS. CAPRICORN MUST ACKNOWLEDGE BOTH SIDES OF ITS CHARACTER AND GET THEM WORKING TOGETHER.

feel comfortable in a country with a strict social code, such as India, where the caste system still largely dictates who can marry whom, or Japan with its complicated codes of social behaviour. In fact, many Capricorns will quite often feel happy in an arranged marriage and even when Capricorn makes its own choices, it may filter its feelings through considerations such as whether it can afford to get married. Romantics may mock, but often a Capricorn relationship weathers the storms better than others.

Another, important feature of Capricorn in its relationships is its element – Earth, which symbolises a love of sensual enjoyment. This aspect of the sign is not always apparent. Its innate conservatism may lead it to disapprove of the pleasures of the flesh, but if Capricorn can find a balance between caution and passion, its relationships can be greatly enriched.

star gazing

OVER 2000 YEARS AGO IT WAS PREDICTED THAT WHEN ALL SEVEN KNOWN PLANETS CONGREGATED IN CAPRICORN, THE WORLD WOULD BE DESTROYED BY FLOOD. IN 1989 THERE WAS A VERY RARE CONJUNCTION OF SATURN, URANUS AND NEPTUNE IN CAPRICORN. THIS COINCIDED NOT WITH A MASSIVE, WORLDWIDE FLOOD, BUT WITH THE DRAMATIC COLLAPSE OF MUCH OF THE COMMUNIST WORLD.

Capricorn's relationships with the Air signs – Libra, Gemini and Aquarius – are an attraction of opposites. Capricorn's entire approach to life is based on achieving practical results, whereas Air signs believe that what people think is often more important than what they do. Capricorn shares with Libra a liking for a well-regulated and ordered existence, but in relationships with independent-minded Gemini and rebellious Aquarius, its

life-enhancing strategies

- Being conservative sometimes means that you miss out on life. Just for a change, try to break the mould. If you normally enjoy classical concerts, go to a rave; if you usually stay in the best hotels, try camping.

- You hang on to old possessions not because you need them, but because they provide a link with the past. You might find it liberating to imagine you are a Sagittarian and get rid of some of this accumulation. Starting with your clothes, check the contents of your cupboards and drawers and put aside anything you have not worn in the last twelve months. As soon as possible, take it all to your local charity shop. Try not to look back.

- You always do best when you follow the path of moderation but whereas you are careful in your eating and drinking, your strong sense of duty sometimes makes you work too hard. Try not to turn into a workaholic and you should feel less stressed.

- Although you prefer to follow a routine in your life, make sure the routine serves you, not the other way round. If you feel trapped by it, try varying it or taking a day off.

- When a relationship comes to an end, give yourself a chance to grieve and deal with the emotional fall-out.

- Your natural caution can be a positive, helping you decide what is achievable in life.

- You think emotions are untidy things, to be kept under control, so are often reluctant to express them. But remember the fish tail on your Capricorn goat, and what it says about your emotional depths. Your feelings are as strong as anyone else's. Showing them does not mean that you have to be slushily romantic.

reluctance to change can cause stress. For the relationship to work Air needs to acknowledge Capricorn's ability to provide security, while Capricorn must respect Air's yearning for freedom.

Capricorn and Water can be a fine combination, good for lasting relationships. The Water signs provide inspiration and emotional warmth, while Capricorn supplies the skill in handling everyday affairs that Water sometimes shies away from. Capricorn and Cancer, being opposite signs, can perfectly balance each other's strengths and weaknesses, and their relationships can be very close. Cancer provides emotional warmth, which makes up for Capricorn's shyness, while Capricorn's business-like instincts compensate for Cancer's unworldliness. With Scorpio and Pisces the bond is likely to be less intense, but if the friendship turns to animosity, the results will be less hostile than between Capricorn and Cancer. Capricorn-Water relationships can come unstuck if Capricorn starts to find Water too emotional and intense or if Water finds Capricorn overcautious and insensitive.

Capricorn can offer the three Fire signs – Aries, Leo and Sagittarius – the material security that leaves them free to pursue their dreams, but relationships between Capricorn and these signs are delicately balanced. Capricorn must accept that, like itself, Aries is deeply ambitious and often self-interested, that Leo might sometimes behave like a prima donna, and that Sagittarius can be here one moment and gone the next! These relationships work when the differences are valued, but they fail if Capricorn's caution clashes with Fire's impatience.

Capricorn's relationships with other Capricorns are naturally stable for they all set great store on the practicalities of living together. These are relationships based on companionship and friendship, the pleasure

that is taken in shared activities and the love that grows and deepens year by year. When it comes to the other Earth signs, Taurus shows Capricorn how to enjoy life's many pleasures, while Capricorn encourages Taurus to make the most of its material resources. When Capricorn gets together with Virgo, Virgo takes care of the details that Capricorn overlooks, while Capricorn offers Virgo social status and respect – all of which, of course, can be seen as necessary for building a happy and fulfilled life together.

Capricorn's health and wellbeing

In medical astrology Capricorn rules the knees, and through its ruling planet, Saturn, which represents structures and boundaries, is linked to the entire skeleton and the skin – everything that holds the human body together. Thus Capricorn generally knows its limits and will lead a healthy lifestyle, not overeating or drinking too much. Neither though, is it likely to be a fitness fanatic. It prefers a good, solid way of life, following a sensible diet and taking a moderate amount of exercise. Hopefully Capricorn should steer clear of problems caused by self-indulgence.

But the connection with the skeleton means that Capricorn is also linked to the joints in general and so it can be susceptible to arthritic or rheumatic problems. Ideally, it should steer clear of activities that might damage the joints, and especially rough sports such as karate and rugby. If it is looking for a way of unwinding, it will enjoy having a massage and it could even consider training to become a masseur. Giving a massage might not sound much like exercise, but it requires more strength and sensitivity than you would imagine. It also helps the giver to relax. Focusing your attention on someone else for an hour soon takes your mind off your own concerns.

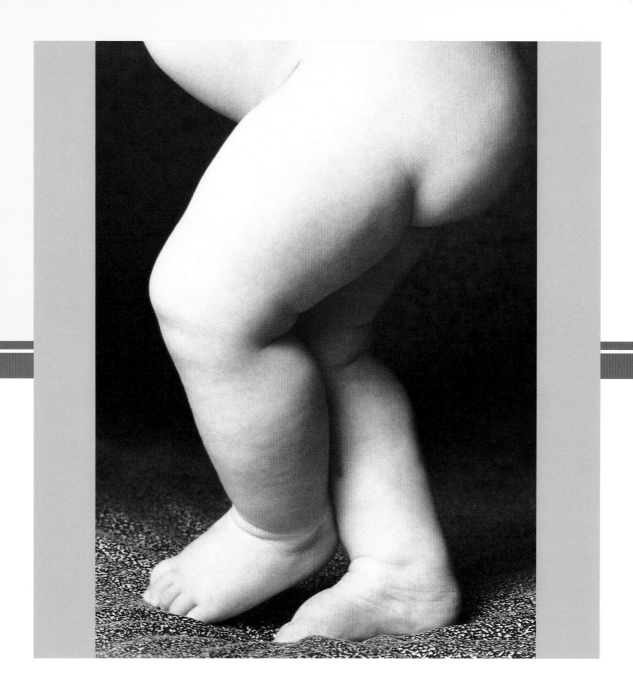

Some Capricorn remedies are good for the bones. Comfrey is known in folklore as 'knit bone', thanks to its supposed ability to heal fractured and broken bones, while the Capricorn mineral salt is Calcium Phosphate, and calcium, as is well known, helps build bones and teeth.

At home, Capricorn likes surroundings that are in keeping with its conservative character and its respect for tradition. It will revel in old-fashioned décor in muted colours and will enjoy filling its home with expensive, antique furniture and objects. All these contribute to its feeling of wellbeing. Capricorn works hard to hold the different aspects of its life together – children, partners, friends, work, finances – and its ideal home will reflect its success in these areas, its status in society and its prosperity. In short, it will emanate a sense of security.

festivals

The great Capricorn calendar festivals come from the

Mediterranean and Middle East, but once had particular meaning

in northern Europe where midwinter, when the earth froze and livestock died, could

be a fearful time. It is no surprise then, that people took every advantage to bring warmth and colour into their

lives at this harsh season.

The Romans celebrated midwinter with abandon. Their festival of Saturnalia, named after Saturn, began on

17 December, continued through the winter solstice on 21 December and climaxed on 29 December with the

Sigillaria, a day when children were given presents. Normal life came to a halt for the whole twelve days as

people enjoyed wild parties and carnivals, dressed up, and exchanged special gifts. The festival was presided

over by a young man who was chosen to be the Lord of Misrule. He was given the freedom to do whatever he

wanted and would also encourage others to break the normal rules of behaviour. Slaves were even sometimes

take a leaf from capricorn

GOOD MANNERS AND CONSIDERATION FOR OTHERS ARE QUALITIES THAT MANY NOW REGARD AS A THING OF THE PAST, BUT THEY ARE OFTEN INBRED IN A CAPRICORNIAN. YOU COULD TRY INCORPORATING SOME GOOD, OLD-FASHIONED COURTESY INTO YOUR EVERYDAY LIFE. REMEMBER TO SAY PLEASE AND THANK YOU, GIVE UP YOUR SEAT ON BUSES AND TRAINS TO THE ELDERLY OR TO PEOPLE STRUGGLING WITH SMALL CHILDREN, DRIVE WITHIN THE SPEED LIMIT AND DON'T LOSE YOUR TEMPER, CALL FRIENDS OR WORK COLLEAGUES TO LET THEM KNOW IF YOU ARE GOING TO BE LATE FOR MEETINGS, DON'T FORGET BIRTHDAYS AND ANNIVERSARIES.

YOU MAY BE SURPRISED HOW EACH LITTLE COURTESY HELPS TO OIL THE WHEELS OF LIFE.

allowed to order their masters around. On 25 December in the northern hemisphere, days begin to be noticeably longer than nights, so the Romans saved this date for their great feast, that of Sol Invictus (the Unconquered Sun). Over the years, the festival of Sol Invictus became one of the Romans' most important religious festivals, until it was borrowed by the Christians for their Christmas Day. The first record of this taking place is in 336 A.D., shortly after the Emperor Constantine legalised Christianity. Constantine, like many early Christians, was a keen advocate of Sol Invictus, and saw the Sun – like Christ – as a symbol of God's light. It was therefore quite natural for early Christians to merge the celebrations of the Sun's rebirth with those for the birth of Christ. And for those of us living through the cold months of winter, Christmas still brings some warmth – spiritual and physical.

a meditation

CAPRICORN IS A VERY CAUTIOUS SIGN. SOME WOULD SAY OVERCAUTIOUS. HOWEVER, WHILE CAUTION CAN ARISE FROM PERFECTLY JUSTIFIABLE FEARS ABOUT THE FUTURE, SOMETIMES CAPRICORN EXAGGERATES THOSE FEARS. AT TIMES LIKE THESE, WHAT CAPRICORN NEEDS MOST IS REASSURANCE THAT, IF IT FOLLOWS A PARTICULAR COURSE OF ACTION, EVERYTHING WILL WORK OUT IN THE END. THIS MEDITATION IS DESIGNED TO GIVE THAT REASSURANCE.

Find somewhere comfortable to sit – a deep sofa or armchair are ideal. Close your eyes and breathe deeply.

Remember what a strong sign Capricorn is. It is a Cardinal sign, capable of controlling its environment. Think

about a problem that you have at present, especially one that is exacerbated by a lack of confidence and by the

constellation

CAPRICORN IS ONE OF THE SMALLEST CONSTELLATIONS. TO
SPOT IT, LOOK AT THE SKY BETWEEN SUNSET AND MIDNIGHT IN
JULY OR AUGUST AND FIND THE THREE BRIGHT CONSTELLATIONS OF THE
'SUMMER TRIANGLE' — AQUILA THE EAGLE, LYRE THE LYRE AND CYGNUS THE
SWAN. NOW LOOK TO THE LEFT AND DOWN SLIGHTLY (OR TO THE RIGHT AND
UP SLIGHTLY IF YOU ARE IN THE SOUTHERN HEMISPHERE), AND YOU WILL BE
GAZING STRAIGHT AT CAPRICORN. IT LOOKS LIKE A LARGE, SMILING
MOUTH — A HAPPIER IMAGE THAN ITS SERIOUS
GOAT-FISH SYMBOL WOULD SUGGEST.

capricorn urges us all to work in the real world and do our duty

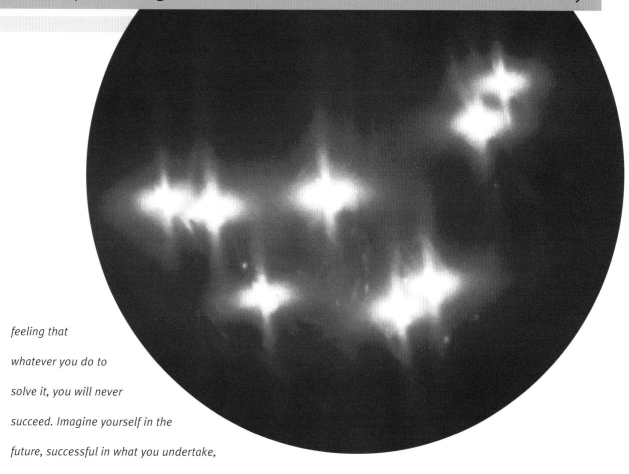

feeling that whatever you do to solve it, you will never succeed. Imagine yourself in the future, successful in what you undertake, reaching the finishing post and obtaining the reward. See that there is nothing to stop you from achieving your goals except your own failure to believe in yourself. Once you have realised that you can succeed, you will be motivated to make a start at tackling the problem.

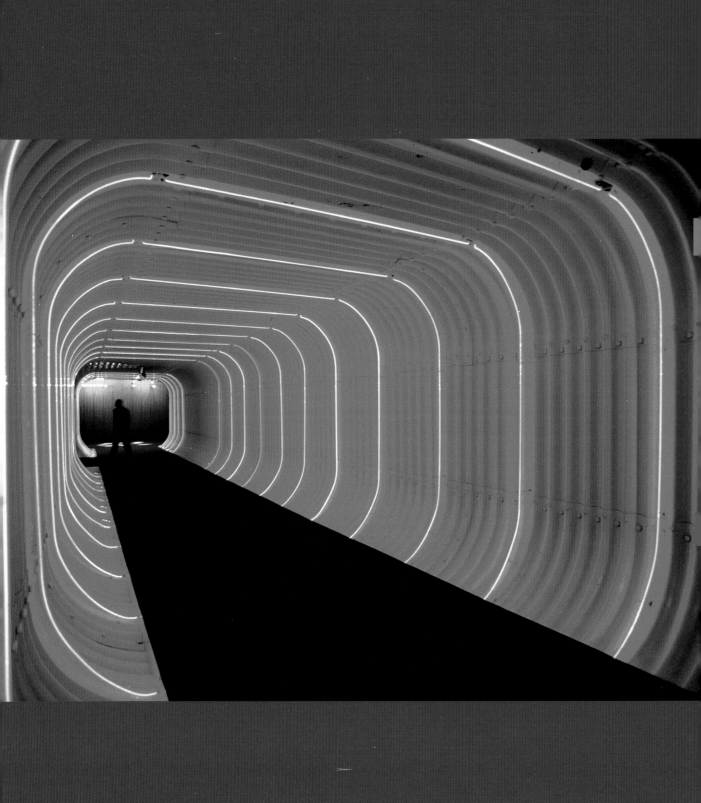

aquarius

fixed, air, male

21 january – 19 february

AQUARIUS IS THE WATER-POURER, THE IDEALIST WHO HOPES TO SPREAD KNOWLEDGE AND SO CREATE A BETTER WORLD. ITS STRENGTHS ARE ITS INVENTIVE GENIUS AND ITS STRONGLY HELD IDEALS. THESE MAKE IT THE SIGN OF THE PHILANTHROPIST, THE PHILOSOPHER AND THE REVOLUTIONARY. ITS WEAKNESSES ARE ITS FAILURE TO UNDERSTAND ITS EMOTIONS AND ITS REFUSAL TO COMPROMISE WITH SIGNS THAT DO NOT SHARE ITS VISION. IT NEEDS TO BE MORE ADAPTABLE AND UNDERSTANDING OF OTHERS AND TO TRY TO PERSUADE THEM OF THE JUSTICE OF ITS CAUSE. IN OTHER WORDS, IT NEEDS TO LEARN TO CO-OPERATE! WHEN IT FINDS A MIDDLE WAY, IT MAY SUCCEED IN PUTTING ITS IDEAS INTO PRACTICE.

AQUARIAN MYTHS OFTEN CONCERN GREAT FLOODS. ACCORDING TO THE BIBLE STORY OF NOAH AND THE ARK, GOD TOLD NOAH HIS PLANS TO DESTROY THE WORLD BY FLOOD AND INSTRUCTED HIM TO SAVE HIS FAMILY AND TWO OF EACH ANIMAL.

A SOUTH AMERICAN FLOOD MYTH TELLS THE STORY OF TWO BROTHERS WHO SURVIVED A SIMILAR FLOOD BY FINDING SHELTER ON TOP OF A TALL MOUNTAIN. WHEN THE WATER RECEDED, ONE OF THE BROTHERS MARRIED A BIRD-GOD AND FOUNDED THE CANARI INDIANS.

SOME AUSTRALIAN ABORIGINES TELL OF A GREAT FLOOD THAT WIPED OUT MOST OF THE WORLD DURING THE DREAMTIME. EVERYONE WAS DROWNED EXCEPT FOR A BOY AND A GIRL WHO HELD ON TO A KANGAROO'S TAIL AND WERE CARRIED TO HIGHER GROUND. WHEN THE FLOOD WATER SUBSIDED, THE TWO SURVIVING CHILDREN STARTED A NEW GENERATION.

THESE AQUARIAN MYTHS ALL DERIVE FROM AQUARIUS'S SYMBOL, THE WATER-POURER. THEY DEAL WITH THE IDEA OF A WICKED WORLD THAT IS CLEANSED OF IMPURITY AND OF A NEW, SINLESS GENERATION THAT ARISES ONCE THE FLOOD WATERS HAVE ACHIEVED GOD'S AIM. BECAUSE OF THE CONNECTION WITH AQUARIUS, ASTROLGERS INFER THAT IT IS AQUARIUS'S TASK TO CLEANSE THE WORLD. BUT ON A MORE PERSONAL LEVEL, AQUARIUS'S RULERSHIP BY SATURN MEANS THAT IT CAN SOMETIMES GET STUCK IN THE PAST. WHEN IT FINDS ITSELF IN A RUT — PERHAPS CAUGHT UP IN AN UNSATISFACTORY RELATIONSHIP — IT WOULD DO WELL TO MAKE SOME DRAMATIC CHANGES IN ITS LIFE. MAYBE IT EVEN NEEDS TO COMPLETELY REINVENT ITSELF. IF IT DOES NOT, IT MAY WELL FIND THAT FATE STEPS IN AND TAKES A HAND, JUST AS IT DID WITH THOSE GREAT FLOODS IN MYTHOLOGY.

idealist
stubborn
revolutionary
confrontational
unpredictable
conservative
technophile
opinionated
eccentric
wacky

pink, electric blue, lead

Aquarius is a sign of contradictions but part of its charm is that one never quite knows what it is going to do next. Astrologers explain this by pointing out that its traditional planetary ruler is Saturn, but that nineteenth-century astrologers added a second ruler, Uranus. The two planets are very different. Uranus represents revolution, rebellion and uncompromising individuality; it loves to innovate, values youth and is prepared to take risks. Saturn, on the other hand, is the arch-conservative, the respecter of old age, order and experience, and the symbol of conformity, traditional values and hard work.

Uranus is also said to symbolise democracy, hence Aquarius, too, is supposed to believe in democratic values. However, with Saturn standing for authority and law and order, the Aquarian version of democracy is often paradoxical – Aquarius demands the freedom to do as it pleases, but sometimes denies others the same. In fact, the perfect Aquarian motto might well be 'Do what I say, not do what I do'. Thus Aquarius is often supposed to be concerned with the collective good, yet it often seems to be pursuing its own interests – rather as Leo does – and failing to take other people's feelings into account.

The fact that the month of January is named after Janus is a further symbol of Aquarius's paradoxical behaviour. Janus was the god of doorways and boundaries and had two faces, one gazing at the past, the other looking to the future. And this is how it is with Aquarius – one foot stuck in a rut, the other always on the move!

Aquarius's classification as both an Air sign and a Fixed sign tells us even more about its nature. As an Air sign, it values facts and information, loves to think and enjoys communicating. Together with Gemini and Sagittarius,

saturn
& uranus

AQUARIUS IS RULED BY SATURN AND, SINCE THE NINETEENTH
CENTURY, ALSO BY URANUS, A PLANET WITH AN UNUSUAL ROTATION
AND AN ECCENTRIC ORBIT. URANUS WAS DISCOVERED IN 1781, JUST AFTER
THE AMERICAN REVOLUTION, SHORTLY BEFORE THE START OF THE FRENCH
REVOLUTION, AND IN THE MIDDLE OF THE INDUSTRIAL REVOLUTION. HENCE
ITS ASSOCIATIONS WITH CHANGE AND INNOVATION. ASTROLOGERS NOWADAYS
PAY MORE ATTENTION TO AQUARIUS'S RADICAL URANIAN INSTINCTS
THAN THEY DO TO ITS SATURNINE FONDNESS FOR LAW AND ORDER.
BUT A TRUE AQUARIAN MAY BE A COMPLEX MIXTURE OF THE
TWO — WANTING TO TRY ANYTHING NEW, BUT WITH A
DEEP RESPECT FOR TRADITION AND LAW
AND ORDER.

it represents inventors, teachers, journalists, philosophers and writers. But as a Fixed sign, Aquarius tends to be stubborn, resistant to change and unwilling to compromise. When it is sticking to its principles, that can be a very good thing, but there are times when Aquarius should try to be more flexible, accept advice from others and find common ground that will bring benefits for all.

Aquarian Sun sign people, past and present, include Mozart, James Joyce, Eartha Kitt, Gertrude Stein, Lord Byron, Zsa Zsa Gabor, Lewis Carroll, James Dean, Abraham Lincoln, Jacqueline du Pré, Charles Dickens, Ronald Reagan, Paul Newman, Vanessa Redgrave, Mia Farrow and Yoko Ono.

Aquarius's relationships

Aquarius's popularity can often be put down to the sign's individualistic and sometimes anarchic qualities, but while some people are fascinated by the eccentric, sometimes wild and wacky behaviour of the classic Aquarian, others are irritated by what they see as the sign's selfishness and egotism. Whatever the type of relationship, life will never be dull with an Aquarian, for Aquarius is always stirring up its more complacent companions, obliging friends to question their own behaviour and turning accepted ideas inside out.

Like some of the other signs, Aquarius has preconceived ideas about how a relationship should work and about the best way for people to behave towards each other. Thus, like Capricorn, it believes in polite manners and

IN ANCIENT CULTURES, WATER WAS SAID TO REPRESENT HUMANITY'S POTENTIAL TO IMPROVE ITSELF AND CREATE A BETTER WORLD. THE SYMBOL OF AQUARIUS IS A MAN OR WOMAN POURING WATER FROM A JAR, HENCE AQUARIANS ARE SUPPOSED TO BE THOSE WHOSE ROLE IT IS TO SPREAD IDEAS AND BE IN THE FOREFRONT OF NEW THINKING. IN THEIR EVERYDAY LIVES, AQUARIANS ARE OFTEN WILLING TO EMBRACE NEW IDEAS AND ARE USUALLY HAPPY TO TRY OUT ANY NEW GIZMO OR GIMMICK.

old-fashioned traditions of hospitality – with Aquarius, standards will never be allowed to slip. But like Libra, Aquarius sometimes tries to fit its partners into a mould and not surprisingly, this can cause problems in their relationships.

And while Aquarius has many friends, there may be few with whom it is really close – it is often said that it loves people but steers clear of intimacy. Sometimes it is criticised for being cold and unemotional. This may be because it is an Air sign and a believer in reason. It is not that it does not care or lacks compassion, but is thinking too much about how it can show its emotions without risking rejection or causing embarrassment to others. As a thinker, it sees the problems that unrestrained passion can cause, the way in which, when people fall wildly in love, the result can be chaos and heartbreak. And so it concludes that it can be safer to go it alone in life.

Of its relationships, those with other Aquarians are often the most straightforward, mainly because they share a rational outlook on life. The trouble is that between them, two Aquarians can easily explain away concepts such as romantic love altogether and can miss out on the fun that romance can bring to a relationship. When it comes to relationships with the other Air signs, those between Aquarius and Gemini can be very enjoyable, but they can come unstuck if the two fail to acknowledge deep, tempestuous feelings when they arise. Libra and Aquarius are the most different, for while Aquarius is happiest doing what it pleases, Libra is happiest doing what other people want. As long as, in general, they see eye-to-eye everything will be fine, but Aquarius can be frustrated by Libra's caution and Libra can be dismayed by Aquarius's rugged individuality.

life-enhancing strategies

- AQUARIUS HAS PLENTY OF FRIENDS BUT SOMETIMES PREFERS TO HANDLE DIFFICULT ISSUES ON ITS OWN. THEN, WHEN IT HAS DOUBTS, IT PANICS. USE YOUR NETWORK OF FRIENDS AND ALLIES TO HELP YOU THROUGH THE STICKY MOMENTS.

- WITH YOUR LOVE OF CHANGE AND INNOVATION, YOU SOMETIMES TAKE THINGS TOO FAR. TRY FOLLOWING THE OLD SAYING, 'IF IT AIN'T BROKE, DON'T FIX IT', AND ONLY MAKE CHANGES IF THEY WILL GENUINELY BRING BENEFITS.

- IF YOU ARE A SATURNINE, SERIOUS-MINDED SORT OF AQUARIAN, SET ASIDE A LITTLE TIME TO GO WILD JUST ONCE IN A WHILE. AND IF YOU ARE AN UNDISCIPLINED FOLLOWER OF URANUS, TRY TO SPEND A WEEK FOLLOWING A STRICT NINE-TO-FIVE ROUTINE.

- YOU BELIEVE IN EQUALITY AND LIKE TO IMAGINE WE ARE ALL AS GOOD AS ONE ANOTHER, BUT IN YOUR HEART YOU DO NOT ALWAYS TRUST OTHER PEOPLE TO DO THINGS FOR YOU. AND YOU ARE OFTEN TOO PROUD TO ASK FOR HELP ANYWAY. TRY TO TRUST PEOPLE AND SHARE THE RESPONSIBILITY FOR GETTING A TASK DONE. IF YOU DON'T, YOU WILL HAVE TO BEAR THE WHOLE BURDEN YOURSELF.

- YOU ARE VERY AWARE OF JUST HOW UNIQUE YOU ARE, BUT SOMETIMES YOU TREAT EVERYONE ELSE AS IF THEY WERE JUST PART OF A SINGLE, HOMOGENOUS MASS. REMEMBER THAT OTHER PEOPLE ARE INDIVIDUALS TOO.

- REMEMBER THAT AS AN AIR SIGN YOU ARE A COMMUNICATOR, BUT YOU CAN BE OVERBLUNT AND SHOULD BEAR IN MIND THAT TOO MUCH HONESTY CAN OFFEND THE SENSITIVE.

- DO NOT OVERANALYSE OR SEEK EXPLANATIONS FOR A LOVED ONE'S EMOTIONS. INSTEAD, JUST LISTEN, SYMPATHISE AND OFFER SUPPORT AND REASSURANCE.

The Earth signs – Taurus, Virgo and Capricorn – offer Aquarius security but also challenge it to put its dreams into practice. Taurus can be closest with Aquarius – sometimes they have an instinctive understanding of one another's needs. Aquarius and Virgo will have a wonderful relationship as long as they bear in mind their differences and sometimes keep their distance. Aquarius's anarchic tendencies can fascinate Virgo but if they live together, Virgo may find them disturbing. Meanwhile, Aquarius likes Virgo's cool efficiency, but can sometimes take it for granted. Aquarius and Capricorn get on well as long as Aquarius provides the excitement and Capricorn keeps the details of everyday life running smoothly, but when they grow apart, Aquarius blames Capricorn for standing in the way of the fulfilment of its dreams, while Capricorn loses faith in Aquarius's ability to get things done.

Aquarius-Fire relationships work very well when each partner shares the other's enthusiasms. When Aquarius gets together with Leo, the results can be electrifying – the two are often instantly and compulsively attracted to each other. The converse is that dislike between them can be equally strong, and when the two fall out, the

results can be very public. What they need is to give each other more space and when problems do arise, try to find practical solutions. Relationships between Aquarius and Aries are often based on companionship rather than passion. That does not mean that they cannot experience passion or fall in love, just that they may prefer being best, lifelong friends. If they drift apart it is usually because they have got all they can from each other and it is time to search for pastures new. Aquarius and Sagittarius are both freedom-loving adventurers. Their relationships thrive as long as they are pursuing the same ambitions in the same place at the same time.

Relationships with the three Water signs can be close. Pisces and Aquarius are not normally considered compatible, but often share a sense of the absurd way the other signs do things, as well as a willingness to wander off the beaten track. Scorpio's intense emotions can prove volatile in combination with Aquarius's powerful dreams, while Aquarius's sharp edge often appeals to the mischievous and argumentative side of Cancer.

Aquarius's health and wellbeing

In medical astrology, Aquarius governs the ankles and these are often the weak point in its anatomy, but its status as a thinking Air sign means that most of its health problems stem from its nerves. With so many thoughts and ideas buzzing around in its brain, Aquarius often suffers a sort of intellectual overload and then easily succumbs to tension. Once this has happened, it sometimes finds it impossible to think consistently, let alone put its plans into practice.

There are many ways Aquarians can find to deal with nervous tension. One favourite is to do meditation and relaxation exercises, but if Aquarius simply cannot stop its thoughts wandering, it could try playing soothing music and allowing its mind to do nothing more than follow the melody. Regular massages also bring enormous benefits to mind and body, but another alternative is a really strong physical workout – vigorous exercise is great for getting rid of nervous tension.

Even though Aquarius, being an individualist, is not much of a team player, it still likes to feel that it is part of a group. If it has a chance to shine, it will be happy being in a team but otherwise, it may well enjoy walking with friends or going to the gym with work colleagues. Given that Aquarius is attracted to the unusual, oriental exercise disciplines may be exactly what it wants. These range from martial arts such as judo, kendo and karate to more sedate practices, such as yoga, t'ai chi and qi gong. Aquarius likes to pick and choose from as many exercise options as possible from all over the world. Eventually it will settle for the one that it finds distinctive and which will suit its own unique needs.

Aquarius's attitude to food, like the sign itself, is often paradoxical. Sometimes it treats food as an irrelevance, a necessary evil and a distraction from the more exciting things in life. Then it will view the physical body as an encumbrance that gets tired and is susceptible to disease, and it will live on junk food, eating while on the move and snacking instead of sitting down for a square meal. But at other times, Aquarius becomes so interested in what it eats that it will start experimenting – a high-protein diet one day, vegan the next, ethnic food from some far-flung part of the world on the following. There's no telling what it will do next.

One of the best remedies for Aquarian tension is a soothing environment. According to Saturn, one of the sign's rulers, the Aquarian home should be decorated in dark colours, but Uranus, the other ruler, suggests electric blues and pinks. But these colours are about as unrelaxing as you could find, so Aquarius should perhaps opt for pastel shades of these colours instead. What Aquarius really needs though, is a special corner to relax in and that means none of the technology – the mobile phones, fax machines and computers – that the sign loves!

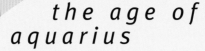

the age of aquarius

ACCORDING TO SOME, THE WORLD IS ABOUT TO ENTER A NEW AGE OF PEACE,
EQUALITY AND HARMONY — THE AGE OF AQUARIUS. SUCH PEOPLE BELIEVE THAT
HISTORY IS DIVIDED INTO PERIODS OF AROUND 2160 YEARS, EACH OF WHICH IS ONE-
TWELFTH OF A CYCLE OF 26,000 YEARS. DURING THIS TIME, THE STARS MAKE A COMPLETE
CYCLE THROUGH THE SKY IN RELATION TO THE SIGNS OF THE ZODIAC. WHEN THE SPRING
EQUINOX TAKES PLACE IN THE CONSTELLATION OF AQUARIUS, THE AGE OF AQUARIUS WILL BEGIN.

UNFORTUNATELY, NOBODY CAN DECIDE WHEN THE AGE OF AQUARIUS WILL START! THE CONSENSUS
PUTS IT AT AROUND 400-600 YEARS' TIME. BUT THE DATE WHEN IT IS DUE TO BEGIN IS LESS
IMPORTANT THAN WHAT ALL THIS REVEALS ABOUT OUR CONTINUING NEED TO LOOK TO THE SKIES
FOR SALVATION. BELIEVERS IN THE AGE OF AQUARIUS ARE NOT ENTIRELY PASSIVE, THOUGH, FOR
RENEWAL AND REBIRTH MYTHS, OF WHICH THIS IS ONE, INSIST THAT WE WORK AS HARD AS
WE CAN TO PREPARE FOR THE BETTER FUTURE. AMONG THESE PEOPLE ARE THE EARLY
TWENTIETH-CENTURY MYSTICS ANNIE BESANT, ALICE BAILEY AND RUDOLF
STEINER, WHO PROMOTED MANY EXTREMELY INNOVATIVE IDEAS IN
THE FIELDS OF EDUCATION, PSYCHOLOGY AND
ORGANIC FARMING.

festivals

Aquarius brings new year celebrations, the
most widely observed being Chinese new year.
'Dragons' – the dragon is a symbol of good luck – parade through the streets and gongs are beaten to frighten
away evil demons, but most celebrations take place at home. People buy new clothes, settle debts, resolve
arguments, buy flowers and plants, give gifts of money to children and clean their kitchens. The cleaning of
the kitchen is done because, so it is said, at new year the kitchen god reports back to the higher gods on the
family's behaviour during the year. A clean kitchen will obviously mean a good report, but to encourage the
god to say sweet things, the family rubs honey on the lips of their kitchen-god statue.

The Korean new year begins on the same day as the Chinese. Korean children try to stay up as late as they can,
motivated by the fear that if they fall asleep before midnight, their eyebrows will have turned white by morning!
On New Year's Day, the whole family gives offerings to its ancestors and afterwards, the young people perform
the *sebae*, bowing to their elders both as a mark of respect and to wish them good fortune for the coming year.
This is a ritual that embodies Aquarius's Saturnine respect for age.

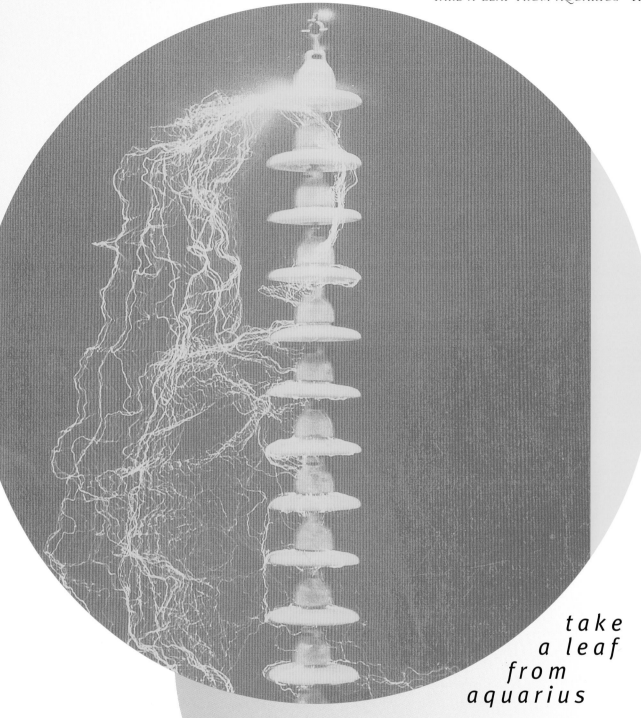

take a leaf from aquarius

Are you one of those people who refuse to find out how to operate a video recorder or a computer? Are you lost when it comes to mini-disc players, DVDs or the internet? You could be missing out on these exciting technological developments, so follow Aquarius's example and make an effort to learn about them and incorporate them in your life. You could find it a transforming experience.

aquarius encourages us to live in the world of ideas

a meditation

AQUARIUS'S RULER, SATURN, OFTEN CAUSES THE SIGN TO SUFFER DOUBTS. THIS MEDITATION IS BASED ON AQUARIUS'S SYMBOL, THE WATER-POURER, AND ON THE IDEA THAT, AS A STREAM FLOWS TO THE SEA IT PASSES THROUGH DIFFERENT LANDSCAPES. THESE SYMBOLISE THE POSSIBILITIES THAT AQUARIUS MEETS IN LIFE. THE MEDITATION IS DESIGNED TO BOOST AQUARIUS'S CONFIDENCE.

Find somewhere quiet to lie or sit. Imagine you are at the top of a mountain. Next to you is a sparkling stream. Now you are lying in the stream. In fact, it feels as if you are the stream. The water cleanses your body and calms your nerves. Gradually the landscape changes from mountain to woodland and then to pasture. The stream turns into a powerful river, pushing everything along with it. You start to feel more powerful, more directed and more aware of how much you can achieve. As the mighty river flows into the ocean, you become conscious of life's limitless possibilities. There are no boundaries except those you set yourself. When you are ready, open your eyes and you will know that you can now tackle goals which you once thought were beyond your grasp.

constellation

THE CONSTELLATION OF AQUARIUS IS RATHER DIFFICULT TO
SEE FOR IT CONTAINS FEW BRIGHT STARS. FIRST, LOCATE THE 'SQUARE'
OF PEGASUS, THE WINGED HORSE, THE FOUR STARS OF WHICH DOMINATE
THE NIGHT SKY IN OCTOBER AND NOVEMBER. THESE ARE EASIER TO SPOT IN
TOWN THAN IN THE COUNTRYSIDE WHERE THE PRESENCE OF SO MANY OTHER
STARS CONFUSES THE PICTURE. ONCE YOU HAVE FOUND PEGASUS, LOOK DOWN
AND TO THE RIGHT — OR TO THE LEFT IF YOU ARE IN THE SOUTHERN
HEMISPHERE — AND YOU WILL BE STARING AT AQUARIUS.

and to be more radical and free thinking

pisces

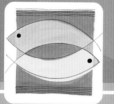

mutable, water, female

20 february – 20 march

PISCES IS THE LAST SIGN IN THE ASTROLOGICAL CALENDAR, THE END OF ALL THINGS, THE COMPLETION AND CULMINATION OF HUMAN EXPERIENCE. IT EMBODIES THE ACCUMULATED ACHIEVEMENTS OF THE PREVIOUS ELEVEN SIGNS, BUT ALSO THEIR MISTAKES. THIS MAKES IT THE WISEST OF THE SIGNS. DRIVEN BY EMOTION, IT IS A SIGN OF LOVE, AND WITH ITS SELFLESSNESS AND IDEALISM, IT IS ALSO A SIGN OF SALVATION, BUT ITS WEAKNESSES ARE CONFUSION, SENTIMENTALITY AND ESCAPISM. THROUGH ITS EXAMPLE, PISCES TEACHES THE OTHER SIGNS THAT MANY OF LIFE'S PROBLEMS ARE UNIMPORTANT. THE REAL WORLD IS THAT OF THE SPIRIT, THE REALM OF MYSTICS, DREAMERS AND VISIONARIES.

MOTIFS OF LOVE AND SALVATION AND THE IMAGE OF THE FISH TYPIFY PISCEAN MYTHS AND LEGENDS. ACCORDING TO ONE ANCIENT GREEK MYTH, THERE WAS A BATTLE BETWEEN THE GODS AND GODDESSES, DURING WHICH ZEUS OVERTHREW HIS FATHER, CRONOS. TO TEACH ZEUS AND HIS FOLLOWERS A LESSON, CRONOS'S WIFE, GAIA, MATED WITH TARTARUS — A GOD OF THE LOWEST UNDERWORLD — AND GAVE BIRTH TO TYPHON, THE MOST AWFUL MONSTER EVER SEEN. TYPHON WREAKED HAVOC WHEREVER IT WENT AND WHEN APHRODITE, GODDESS OF LOVE, SAW IT APPROACHING, SHE TOOK REFUGE WITH HER SON EROS ON THE BANKS OF THE EUPHRATES. FEARFUL THAT TYPHON WOULD FIND THEM, THEY JUMPED INTO THE RIVER. THEY WERE SAVED BY TWO FISH WHO CARRIED THEM UP TO HEAVEN.

A BIBLE STORY RELATES HOW GOD TOLD JONAH TO WARN THE WICKED PEOPLE OF NINEVEH THAT HE WOULD DESTROY THEM. LACKING COURAGE TO DO GOD'S WILL, JONAH RAN AWAY TO SEA, HE WAS SWEPT OVERBOARD IN A STORM AND EATEN BY A WHALE. WHEN THE WHALE VOMITED HIM UP, JONAH FINALLY DELIVERED HIS MESSAGE. THE PEOPLE PRAYED TO BE SAVED AND GOD ANSWERED THEIR PRAYERS.

PISCES TENDS TO RUN AWAY FROM AWKWARD ISSUES — LIKE APHRODITE TRYING TO ESCAPE FROM TYPHON — AND TO PRETEND THAT PROBLEMS WILL GO AWAY IF THEY ARE IGNORED — JUST AS JONAH HOPED TO AVOID HAVING TO DELIVER HIS FATEFUL MESSAGE TO THE PEOPLE OF NINEVEH. HOWEVER, AS JONAH FOUND OUT, PROBLEMS USUALLY CATCH UP WITH YOU IN THE END AND, LIKE THE MONSTER TYPHON, MIGHT LEAVE BEHIND A TRAIL OF DESTRUCTION. BUT SINCE PISCES IS A SIGN OF LOVE, IT IS FITTING THAT IN THE MYTH, THE GODDESS OF LOVE SHOULD ESCAPE THE DREADFUL MONSTER.

kind
vague
mystical
indecisive
changeable
compassionate
manipulative
responsive
reflective
creative

turquoise, blues, sea-green, tin

Pisces is a Water sign – an emotional, romantic dreamer. It is also a Mutable sign and so possesses a changeable nature. In fact, it is so changeable that it often starts one task then goes on to another at the slightest distraction, leaving the old tasks half finished. Pisces' changeability also derives from Jupiter, its ruling planet. In ancient legends, the god Jupiter would change into a person or animal in order to pursue his sexual conquests. Like Jupiter, Pisces can subtly adapt its personality to suit its circumstances, and for this reason it is sometimes known as the chameleon of the zodiac.

Another aspect of Pisces' changeability is its willingness – rather like Libra's – to agree with the last person it spoke to. In other words, it can be infinitely flexible. However, some see this as a weakness. They think Pisces doesn't have a will of its own, that it lacks 'backbone' or is a 'wet fish'. But perhaps this is appropriate for, after all, Pisces' sign is based on the fish. The sign is, in fact, represented by two fish swimming in opposite directions, and this can be read as a metaphor for Pisces' tendency to be involved in the spiritual and material worlds at the same time and its ability to pursue opposing courses of action simultaneously. But the fish are usually depicted linked by a single thread, suggesting that opposites are always connected and that one extreme only exists in relation to another. Meanwhile, the sea in which Pisces' fish swim is the world of dreams. To modern psychologists it represents the unconscious mind.

Pisces was not always a fish, though. The ancient Babylonians saw it as two groups of stars in the sky – *kun mes*, the tail, and *sim mah*, the swallow. Some people joined the two to make the 'tails of the swallow'. The thought of Pisces flying with the clouds, soaring to the heights and seeing the whole world spread out before its

jupiter & neptune

PISCES SHARES ITS PLANETARY RULER, JUPITER, WITH
SAGITTARIUS. JUPITER IS A PLANET OF WISDOM, BUT WHEREAS
IN SAGITTARIUS — A FIRE SIGN — JUPITER IS CONFIDENT AND
OPTIMISTIC, IN PISCES IT REPRESENTS A MORE CONTEMPLATIVE, LESS
IMPULSIVE SORT OF WISDOM.

PISCES ALSO HAS A SECOND PLANETARY RULER — NEPTUNE —
A PLANET DISCOVERED IN 1846. NEPTUNE'S ROLE AS
GOD OF THE DEEP SUMS UP PISCES' ELUSIVE, OTHER-
WORLDLINESS. THE TWO PLANETS COMBINE TO
MAKE PISCEANS SENSITIVE, VISIONARY AND
OFTEN COMPLETELY IMPRACTICAL.

gaze adds a different
perspective to that of the fish who dives to the
depths of the ocean and explores hidden feelings
and the world of dreams.

Pisces' spirituality symbolises visionaries, the men and women who
follow a path of religious renunciation, or artists who reinterpret reality. Many of the mundane details of life that
other people take seriously, Pisces regards as not being of importance in the grand scheme of things, and so it
is perfectly willing to compromise over them – hence its day-to-day flexibility. But when Pisces discovers
a sense of destiny, it will fight for its beliefs against all odds, running the risk of taking itself too seriously and
growing intolerant of others' beliefs in a most un-Piscean manner. And because Pisces is not interested in the
humdrum details of life, it has a reputation for being impractical and lazy. Yet, paradoxically, in certain matters,
especially those of the heart, Pisces is a perfectionist. This can be demoralising, for whatever Pisces achieves,
it often feels it is not good enough. Perhaps that is why it sometimes seems loath to tackle anything.

But there are other, more positive aspects to Pisces. It can be one of the sweetest, kindest and most charming
of signs, but it is extremely sensitive and easily hurt. It readily soaks up other people's emotions and if you
burst into tears, the chances are that the nearest Pisces will as well. As a result, one typical Piscean problem
is that the sign often imagines it has offended someone and will feel guilty about it, frequently without reason.
And since it is easily upset, it often retreats into itself and so appears shy and nervous. This shyness can lead

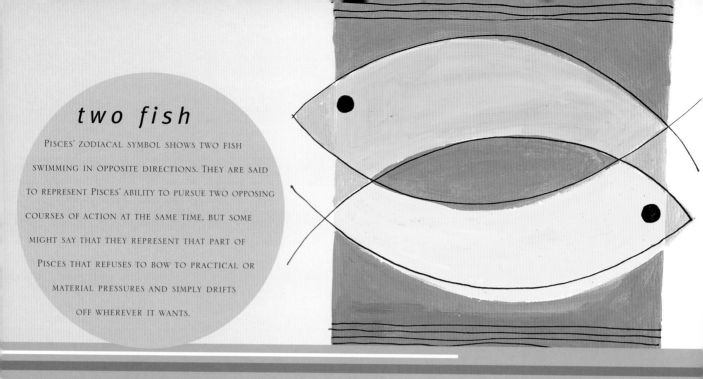

two fish

PISCES' ZODIACAL SYMBOL SHOWS TWO FISH SWIMMING IN OPPOSITE DIRECTIONS. THEY ARE SAID TO REPRESENT PISCES' ABILITY TO PURSUE TWO OPPOSING COURSES OF ACTION AT THE SAME TIME, BUT SOME MIGHT SAY THAT THEY REPRESENT THAT PART OF PISCES THAT REFUSES TO BOW TO PRACTICAL OR MATERIAL PRESSURES AND SIMPLY DRIFTS OFF WHEREVER IT WANTS.

people to think that Pisceans are cold, distant and unemotional, but it is really nothing more than a lack of confidence brought on by past wounds. With an extra helping of love, affection, support and reassurance from friends and family, they will soon come out of themselves.

True to form, the personalities born with the Sun in Pisces include a fair number of dreamers, visionaries and artists, among them Albert Einstein, Michelangelo, George Washington, Frédéric Chopin, Rudolf Nureyev, Patty Hearst, Elizabeth Taylor, Vassili Nijinsky, Liza Minnelli, Ivana Trump, Jean Harlow and Mikhail Gorbachov.

Pisces' relationships

Pisceans bring to their relationships one simple but useful skill: the ability to adapt their behaviour in order to reflect the people they are with. As a result, they are sometimes criticised for trying to be all things to all people, however, psychologists say it is good to mirror other people's behaviour, for this engenders trust and a spirit of compromise and harmony. But the downside is that by mirroring others, Pisces can sometimes lose sight of who it really is and may even overlook the shortcomings of the person it loves. It may eventually discover that the object of its affections is not really worth the trouble, but sometimes this simple fact will escape them completely.

life-enhancing strategies

- As an intuitive person, you often find it difficult to distinguish feelings from fact. Be sure of your facts before you take any decisions that might have serious consequences.

- Keep a grip on the practicalities of life. Set yourself a routine for jobs such as opening letters and paying bills. You do not want to wake up one day and find that the bailiffs have carried your possessions away.

- If you are accused of being lazy, forget that you were born under an ethereal sign. Instead, anticipate the Sun's move into Aries and try setting the pace and getting on with things.

- Do not always blame yourself if plans go wrong and remember that you do not always have to feel responsible for others.

- It is easy to acquire a reputation for incompetence, so only take on things you know you can do, then do them properly and on time.

- Play to your strengths. When loved ones are upset, encourage them to talk and offer them your emotional support and wisdom.

Pisceans are true romantics, engaged on a quest for the perfect partner. It is as though Pisces' two fish are searching for one another but, because they face in opposite directions, keep missing each other. In the real world, of course, the perfect partner does not exist so, sadly, Pisceans are doomed never to find what they are looking for. Their search for perfection also means that they can never live up to their own standards and this can result in a lack of confidence and the feeling that they are unloveable. Self-pity is not a quality that is likely to attract a partner, so Pisces needs to break out of this cycle if it is to find happiness with someone.

Pisces is often attracted to the Water signs because it thinks they understand its feelings better than Fire, Air and Earth do. When two Pisceans get together, surprisingly, the relationship is not always an easy one. Either they hit it off instantly or, as often occurs, each reminds the other of qualities they find embarrassing in themselves and a mutual awkwardness develops which spells doom for the relationship. Pisces gets on most comfortably with the other Water signs – Cancer and Scorpio. Both these signs are romantic and are unlikely to be disturbed by the displays of emotion that are essential to a Pisces. Of the two, Cancer is most likely to form a long-term partnership with Pisces, but if the two drift apart, it can be because of a failure to communicate. Each assumes that the other knows what he or she is feeling – sometimes wrongly. In relationships with Scorpio, Pisces can find Scorpio's

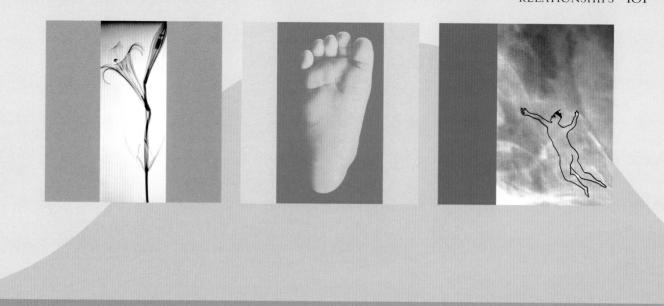

intensity exciting and dangerous, while Scorpio appreciates Pisces' happy-go-lucky qualities, but the two can come unstuck if they brood or sulk rather than facing up to emotional difficulties.

Pisces often looks to the Earth signs for security. Its most intriguing relationships are often with Virgo, who is fascinated by Pisces' imagination, while Pisces is attracted to Virgo's practical skills. If the two fall out, Virgo despairs at Pisces' failure to grasp reality, while Pisces can no longer stand Virgo's fussiness. Friendships with Taurus can be based on a love of life's pleasures, but they may drift apart if Pisces decides it's time for a change while stubborn Taurus wants to stay put. Relationships with Capricorn may be founded on companionship, but if Pisces senses the lack of a deep bond between them, they may be good friends but never lovers.

Relationships with the three Air signs are often lively. Gemini loves Pisces' strange imagination and provides it with a spark of intellectual stimulation and a sense of adventure. Yet sometimes there simply is not enough to hold them together. In relationships with Libra, Libra's love of beauty dovetails neatly with Pisces' sensitivity, but the two may clash if Libra clings to its firm ideas about how life should be lived, while Pisces just wants to follow its feelings. Pisces and Aquarius are not normally considered compatible, but in reality there is often nothing to stop them forming a close friendship. They frequently share a sense of the absurdity of the way that other people do things, and a willingness to wander off the beaten track.

Relationships with the three Fire signs can be stormy. Aries is perhaps the most different to Pisces, and even though the two can share the same passions, their relationships work best when each knows what they have to

do and their responsibilities never overlap. There is often a special magic in Pisces' links with Leo. The two both have a creative imagination and a desire to raise their sights beyond life's ordinary expectations. Pisces and Sagittarius share a sense of idealism and a reluctance to be pinned down. In a relationship, they can well encourage one another to explore new beliefs and lifestyles, but sometimes they simply do not get around to doing the things – like making a home together – that cement a long-term relationship.

Pisces' health and wellbeing

In medical astrology, Pisces rules the feet and so it is said that Pisceans may have flat feet, large collections of shoes and should take up activities such as dancing, which requires nimbleness of the feet. The classic Piscean complimentary remedy is, not surprisingly, reflexology. This is based on the principle that each part of the foot relates to a different region of the body, and that by applying pressure to specific points on the foot, a whole host of ailments can be eased. Failing reflexology, Pisceans will certainly find just a simple foot massage to be extremely therapeutic.

Pisces is the most 'watery' of the Water signs, so we might expect that Pisceans keep fit by swimming and that they enjoy relaxing in a steam bath – and many do. But what Pisceans appreciate in any form of sport is a sense of delicacy and refinement, so dancing – which ties in with Pisces' ruling of the feet – is the perfect way for Pisceans to keep the body in trim. Walking is another classic Piscean exercise: as you walk, your feet are being massaged and this can be regarded as the equivalent of a reflexology session. But when Pisces is walking, he or she should spare no effort in finding the right shoes; if there is a clash between fashion and comfort, comfort should win every time.

It has been observed that people born under this sign sometimes feel as if their body is undermining them or that it is in some way letting them down. They may react to this by overindulging in food and drink or by swinging to the other extreme and falling prey to the latest health fad. It is also said that, in their quest to escape this world and explore other realities, Pisceans are sometimes attracted to drink and drugs. But this is something of a generalisation. What may be true is that Pisceans are more likely than most to be aware that revelations received while under the influence of drink or drugs are no more than illusions.

Pisces is rather vulnerable to stress, not because it is hard-working but because it is sensitive and so less able to tolerate unpleasant or tense situations than many other signs. This means that the perfect Piscean environment is calm and peaceful, with lush vegetation and a view of sky and countryside, preferably near water. Pisces loves luxury, but will not go out of its way to create a luxurious environment for itself. Instead, Pisceans are frequently happy – perhaps out of laziness – to put up with whatever is on offer. They appreciate tidiness but left to their own devices, will live in organised chaos. They also hate to throw anything away, so you often find them living surrounded by mementos from their past. When it comes to its surroundings, Pisces needs to learn a lesson from Virgo – the sign of care and attention to detail. Instead of waiting for someone else to come along and make things perfect, Pisces should get on and do it itself – or risk waiting for ever.

take a leaf from pisces

IN MANY PARTS OF THE WESTERN WORLD,
SPIRITUALITY HAS BEEN REPLACED BY MATERIALISM. WE
SPEND A LOT OF OUR TIME THINKING ABOUT WHAT WE CAN
ACQUIRE NEXT, IMAGINING THAT THIS WILL MAKE US HAPPY, BUT
WE OFTEN FIND THAT ONCE WE HAVE IT, HAPPINESS IS STILL OUT OF
REACH. IF YOU ARE AWARE THAT THIS IS GOING ON IN YOUR LIFE, IT MIGHT
PAY YOU TO REASSSESS THINGS AND TO TRY TO BRING SOME SPIRITUALITY
INTO YOUR LIFE. THIS COULD MEAN GETTING BACK IN TOUCH
WITH RELIGION, SPENDING MORE TIME WITH YOUR FAMILY
AND FRIENDS, OR SIMPLY TAKING TIME TO ADMIRE
THE BEAUTY OF THE WORLD.

festivals

The main themes of Pisces' festivals are renunciation and sacrifice, for Pisces, like Virgo, has a tendency to sacrifice itself for the sake of a relationship, to compromise itself for others.

This is the time of year of the Christian festival of Lent, the forty-day period leading up to Easter. It commemorates the forty days Jesus spent wrestling with the devil in the wilderness before his baptism. Traditionally, Lent is a time to renounce the pleasures of the flesh and to give up something you love, such as meat, alcohol or tobacco. The start of Lent is often, in Catholic countries, the excuse for a carnival – the word 'carnival' comes from the Latin *carne* (meat) and *vale* (farewell). People who observe Lent sometimes donate the money they save during Lent to a charity. Thus the theme of Lent is sacrifice. By giving up at least one pleasure, people are recognising the value of Christ's abstinence in the desert.

Easter follows when the Sun is in the sign of Aries. This festival commemorates the supreme sacrifice, the moment when Christ was crucified and took the sins of the world on his shoulders. Easter, therefore, despite falling with the Sun in Aries, also has Piscean overtones, but the signs of the zodiac often overlap. When Easter takes place, the Sun is often passing through the stars of Pisces!

messiahs

THE PSYCHOLOGIST CARL JUNG
NOTED HOW, FOR CENTURIES, PISCES
WAS ASSOCIATED WITH THE MESSIAH. ONE
FIFTEENTH-CENTURY PORTUGUESE JEWISH SCHOLAR
HAD REMARKED THAT A CONJUNCTION BETWEEN JUPITER
AND SATURN APPEARED IN THE SIGN OF PISCES SHORTLY BEFORE THE BIRTH
OF MOSES — NOT THE MESSIAH, BUT ONE OF JUDAISM'S MOST IMPORTANT PROPHETS. AND IN THE SEVENTEENTH CENTURY,
THE ASTRONOMER JOHANNES KEPLER PUBLISHED HIS THEORY THAT THE SAME ALIGNMENT HAD OCCURRED IN 4 B.C.
AND WAS NONE OTHER THAN THE STAR OF BETHLEHEM, HERALDING THE BIRTH OF CHRIST.
JUNG ALSO NOTED THAT THE FIRST CHRISTIANS USED THE FISH AS THEIR SECRET SYMBOL. THIS WAS PARTLY BECAUSE
JESUS HAD TOLD HIS DISCIPLES THEY WOULD BE 'FISHERS OF MEN', BUT ALSO BECAUSE, ACCORDING TO JUNG,
THOSE CHRISTIANS HAD OBSERVED THAT THE SUN ROSE IN THE STARS OF PISCES AT THE SPRING
EQUINOX. BY CARVING FISH IMAGES IN THEIR CATACOMBS, CHRISTIANS WERE ANNOUNCING
THAT CHRISTIANITY WAS THE RELIGION OF THE NEW ASTROLOGICAL AGE AND
THAT PISCES WAS THE SIGN OF SALVATION.

sensitive and imaginative,

a meditation

PISCES IS SENSITIVE AND OFTEN FINDS IT HARD TO
COPE WITH SETBACKS. THIS CLASSICALLY PISCEAN MEDITATION
IS DESIGNED TO HELP PISCES RESTORE ITS BELIEF IN ITSELF AND ITS FAITH IN THE FUTURE.

Find a quiet space, close your eyes and imagine you are lying on a beach by a calm sea. After a while, you imagine you are floating, perfectly safely, on the water. Now you are deep underwater, yet you still feel safe. You become aware of a light drawing you towards it, coming from a submarine cavern. Part of you wants to enter the cavern, but part of you is hesitant. Be aware of your feelings, even the negative ones. The farther you go, the brighter the light becomes. Now you are at the heart of the cavern and you see that the light comes from a treasure chest. Its lid is open and it is full of wonderful things. You sort through them until you find one that seems full of positive meaning for you. You know it is a talisman that will restore your spirits whenever you feel low. You pick it up and retrace your path, looking around you before you swim towards the surface to make sure you will always know how to find your way back. When you reach land, you may want to draw or model the talisman, or talk about it with your friends. Become aware of the talisman's meaning for you. And be aware that there are more treasures waiting to be brought up from the watery depths that repesent your deeper self.

constellation

THE STARS OF PISCES ARE INVISIBLE IN MARCH BECAUSE THEY ARE OBSCURED BY THE SUN'S BRILLIANCE, YET IN SEPTEMBER THEY CAN BE SEEN SHINING IN THE SKY AT MIDNIGHT, THEIR TWO FISH CONNECTED BY A THIN LINE OF STARS. IT HAS BEEN PROPOSED THAT THE LARGE SIZE OF THE CONSTELLATION IS AN INDICATION OF ITS ENORMOUS AGE. WHEN IT WAS CREATED THERE WERE FEW CONSTELLATIONS AND A LARGE AMOUNT OF SKY TO FILL. THIS IS A PLEASING THEORY, BUT THE EVIDENCE IS SLIGHT. PISCES, THOUGH, WAS NEVER A SIGN THAT WORRIED MUCH ABOUT THE FACTS!

Pisces shows us how to conjure up the future through our dreams

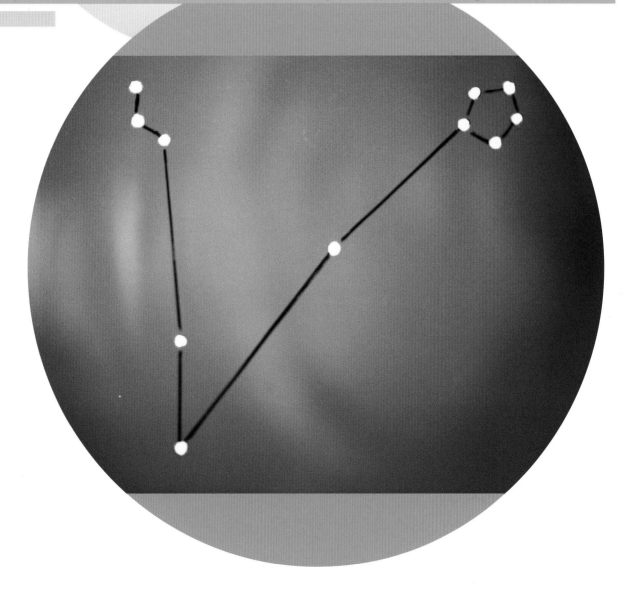

it is the stars,

The stars

PICTURE CREDITS

Library/Joyce Tenneson; 154 centre Photonica/Steve Marsel; 154 right Gettyone Stone/HN5221.001; 155 Photonica/Armen Kachaturian; 156 Gettyone Stone/828518.002; 157 Corbis/Hulton-Deutsch Collection; 158 Photonica/Fujio Matsumoto; 159 Lorry Eason; 160 Photonica/Gyro Photography; 163 Photonica/Katrin Thomas; 164 Gettyone Stone/163P3 Interpretations; 167 above left Photonica/Tommy Flynn; 167 above centre Gettyone Stone/888366.001; 167 above right Photonica/M Kazama; 167 below Corbis/Bettmann; 168 left Gettyone Stone/BC7653.001; 168 centre Photonica/Ellen Carey; 168 right Gettyone Stone/17P1 Interpretations; 169 Gettyone Stone/169P3

from Interpretations; 170 Photonica/Elaine Mayes; 171 Gettyone Stone/HF2227.001; 172 Gettyone Stone/BC9850.001; 174 Photonica/David Hiscock; 177 Photonica/Shusuke Nakamura; 178 Gettyone Stone/BC9116.001; 179 Photonica/Bildhuset AB; 180 Corbis/Hulton-Deutsch Collection; 181 left Gettyone Stone /BC8499.001; 181 centre Gettyone Stone/BC3320.001; 181 right Photonica /Teruhisa Shiozu; 182 left Photonica/Marianne Grondahl; 182 centre Photonica/Peter Murphy; 182 right Gettyone Stone/888248.001; 183 Photonica/Komei Yusa; 184 Photonica/Sally Boon; 185 Gettyone Stone/580101.005; 186 Gettyone Stone/BC8584.001.

The author would like to thank the many people who have played a role, knowingly or otherwise, in the conception of this book. They include Wendy Buonaventura, Nick Bantock, Emma Birt, Simon Bright, Luisa Calderon, Joseph Campbell, Christine Carter, Arabella Churchill, Sue Clayton, David Connearn, Sean Cubitt, Kath Dent, Françoise Dietrich, Michael Eavis, Keith Erskine, Rachel Gibson, Lawrence Golding, Simon Goss, Diana Grace-Jones, Albert Hoffman, Andrew Kerr, David Kestler, Judith Lawrence, Liz Lee, Sean Lovatt, Rebecca Lyle, Ewen McLeod, Hilary Mandleberg, Michael R. Meyer, John Michel, Doreen Montgomery, Tony Morris, John Naylor, Gerard Selby, Jane O'Shea, Martin Parr, Beth Shaw, Ian Wallace, Helen Vivian and Joyce Wyton.

He also extends his grateful acknowledgement to Chester Kemp for devising and providing the Moon Tables.